in French

The all-in-one language and travel guide

Brigitte Rix

Louise Rogers Lalaurie

BBC Books

Developed by BBC Languages
Series Adviser: Derek Utley
Audi producer: John Green, tefl tapes
Concept design by Carroll Associates
Typeset and designed by Book Creation Services, London

Cover design by Carroll Associates
Cover photo: Telegraph Colour Library
Map: Malcolm Porter

ISBN 0 563 40052 8

Published by BBC Books, a division of BBC Worldwide Ltd
First published 1998
Reprinted 2000
Printed and bound in Great Britain by Omnia Books Ltd, Glasgow
Colour separations by DOT Gradations, Chelmsford

Photographs
All photographs by Luke Finn, except the following:

Anthony Blake p61(m), 64(m), 66(t), 70(m), 71(t, m), 84, 85(t), 89
Martin Brigdale p81, 82, 86
Cephas p67(b), 68(m), 69, 72(b), 73, 79(t), 87(l)
Angela Clarence p56(t), 94(t), 98(t), 108(m), 109
Getty Images p29(tr), back (m)
Graham Kirk p76, 78, 79(b), 83, 85(m), 87(r), 88
Life File p1(b), 3(m), 5, 6(t), 7, 8, 13(t), 14(b), 18(t), 20(t), 21, 24,
25(t), 26(t), 27, 29(tl), 49, 51, 52, 54(b), 113
James Murphy p80
Pictor International – London p2, 4, 11, 12, 13(b), 16, 17, 18(b), 19,
20(t), 22, 23, 25(b), 26(b), 28(b), 91(t), back (br)
Glyn Williams spine, back (t)
Stuart Windsor p3(t), 30(br), 35(mr), 41(t), 42(l), 43(br), 45(br), 64(t)
Zefa Pictures p1(t), 9, 10, 14(t), 15, 67(t), 75, 92, 99(t), back (bm)
Due to the scale of the map, it has not been possible to include
full details; however, every care has been taken to include as
many of the places mentioned in the book as possible.

Insider's guide to France | page 1
Introduction
Paris and the Ile de France, Alsace and Lorraine, Lyon and the
surrounding countryside, Côte d'Azur, Provence and Languedoc,
South-west France and Brittany and Normandy
Holidays, festivals and events

Bare necessities | page 30
Essential words and phrases
Numbers, times, days of the week

Getting around | page 37
Travelling around France: car hire and public transport

Somewhere to stay | page 46
Finding accommodation: hotels, self-catering, campsites

Buying things | page 55
Food, clothes, stamps

Café life | page 66
Getting drinks and snacks

Eating out | page 72
Ordering a meal

Menu reader | page 78
Understanding French menus

Entertainment and leisure | page 90
Finding out what's on, getting tickets and information

Emergencies | page 100
Doctors, dentists, chemists, car breakdown, theft

Language builder | page 108
The basics of French grammar

Answers | page 112
Key to Language works and Try it out

Dictionary | page 114
Full list of French words with English translations

Sounds French | inside cover
Simple guide to pronouncing French

INTRODUCTION

Get By in French will enable you to pick up the language, travel with confidence and experience the very best the country has to offer. You can use it both *before* a trip, to pick up the basics of the language and to plan your itinerary, and *during* your trip, as a phrasebook and as a source of practical information in all the key travel situations.

Contents
Insider's guide to France An introduction to the country, a guide to the main cities and region-by-region highlights for planning itineraries.
Bare necessities The absolute essentials of French.
Seven main chapters covering key travel situations from *Getting around* to *Entertainment and leisure*. Each chapter has three main sections: *information* to help you understand the local way of doing things; *Phrasemaker*, a phrasebook of key words and phrases; *Language works/Try it out*, simple dialogues and activities to help you remember the language.
Menu reader A key to menus in French.
Language builder A simple introduction to French grammar.
1000-word dictionary The most important French words you will come across with their English translations.
Sounds French A clear guide to pronouncing the language.

How to use the book
Before you go You can use the *Insider's guide* to get a flavour of the country and plan where you want to go. To pick up the language, the *Phrasemaker* sections give you the key words and phrases; the *Language works* dialogues show the language in action, and *Try it out* offers you a chance to practise for yourself.

During your trip *The Insider's guide* offers tips on the best things to see and do in the main cities. *The Phrasemaker* works as a phrasebook with all the key language to help you get what you want. Within each chapter there is also practical 'survival' information to help you get around and understand the country.

Insider's guide to France

The French take a brisk approach to their large, diverse country. France, to them, is l'Hexagone ('the Hexagon') framed – clockwise – on its six sides by the plains and forests of the north and north-east, the Alps, the Mediterranean, the mountains of the Pyrenees, the Atlantic and la Manche, that narrow stretch of sea keeping England at bay, and which is never, ever, referred to as the English Channel. Like most modern European states, France is a collection of older kingdoms, duchies and peoples, and one that didn't get where it is without a struggle. Relations with its neighbours – Italy (the Romans), England, Spain and Germany – have been marked by invasions and counter-invasions over two millenia. At home, too, there were bloodbaths for anti-Catholic heretics, Protestants and royalists (the Revolution of 1789), colonial wars (notably Algeria in the late 1950s) and student riots in 1968. Since the 1789 revolution France has been an empire, then a monarchy again, then a second republic, another empire, and finally a third, fourth, and fifth republic, the latter with a cherished constitution voted by referendum in 1958 – a triumphant assertion, for many French people, of past troubles overcome.

The French people

There's a definite 'republican' respect in people's daily dealings with each other – shopkeepers, bartenders, waiters and salespeople are consulted as highly trained specialists (which they usually are). They are civil, never servile, and public behaviour is exceedingly polite and formal – a new arrival in the local butcher's queue will greet everyone with a generalised *Messieurs Dames* and receive nods, handshakes or kisses all round.

The French are unafraid of progress – they are enthusiastic technophiles and pro-Europeans, yet their traditional, rather closed, family-based society remains wary of immigrants, and was badly frightened by the student riots of 1968. Avoid brash, showy

Chenonceaux

behaviour and above all speak French. Attempts to communicate in your own tongue will be seen as arrogant (rather than desperate!). Start a conversation in French, and doors may open – an invitation to drinks (*apéritifs*) or to see the family's 300-year-old olive press. This is France's delightful hidden side, and the French language is the key.

Climate

France (say the French) has two climates: north of the river Loire it's cold and wet, while below the Loire things gradually improve down to the hot, sunny south where the year's rain falls in a few storms, frost-free winters are not unusual and there's good weather from March to November. In fact, the weather has its ups and downs right across France – the Paris region can be drizzly and overcast, Atlantic storms buffet the west coast and Provence is regularly scoured by the violent *mistral* wind; spring and autumn are perhaps the best times to visit – pleasantly warm, sunny (and less crowded than in summer) everywhere from Paris to Nice. Winters are milder and shorter than in northern or central Europe, although severe weather can still strike. At the southern tip of the Alps in spring you can ski in the morning, then bask on the beach at Cannes after lunch!

Landscapes and art

French landscapes are synonymous with the artists that have made them world famous. There's the dappled calm of the Seine valley (Monet and Sisley), the olive groves, cypress trees and ochre earth of Provence (Van Gogh and Cézanne), or the vivid colours of the Mediterranean coast (Signac, Derain, Matisse). All the dash and verve of French life is there, too, in Impressionist snapshots of the Parisian scene, Degas' days at the races (and nights at the Opéra), Gauguin's Breton peasants, or Raoul Dufy's affectionate portraits of Paris, Cannes and the Baie des Anges in Nice. Travellers and art-lovers visiting France today will find much unchanged, and much that is still (relatively) undiscovered.

Courchevel, Savoie

Currency/Changing money

France is an affluent country, and prices can be high although hotels, set menus and petrol remain competitive by average European standards. Automatic cash dispensers (often with a choice of languages) are found in all towns and many villages, but may not accept all foreign cards. Most foreign credit cards are accepted in most shops for purchases over 50 or 100 francs. Eurocheques or traveller's cheques may also be accepted.

Banks open from 9 am to 12 noon and from early afternoon to 5 pm, from Tuesday to Saturday. In larger towns, look out for branches of the Banque de France which offers a highly competitive exchange rate and no charges. You

can also change or withdraw cash at a Bureau de Change, often open late or 24 hours a day in Paris, but commission charges are high.

French francs (1F) are divided into 100 centimes. 50 centimes – *cinquante centimes* – is written as 0,50F. There are 5, 10, 20 and 50-centime pieces; 1, 2, 5, 10 and 20-franc pieces, and 20, 50, 100, 200 and 500-franc notes. Look for the tiny yellow spot in the centre of 20-franc coins – they are almost identical to 10-franc coins.

La Roque Gageac, Dordogne

Visas and entry requirements

Citizens of the European Union, the USA, New Zealand and Canada do not need a visa for stays of less than 90 days. Australian and South African citizens must apply for visas (maximum stay three months) at their nearest French consulate, before entering France.

Citizens of Belgium, the Netherlands, Luxemburg, Germany, Spain and Portugal can enter France without a passport. All other visitors will need to present a full passport. For addresses of embassies in France, see p101.

Paris and the Île-de-France

Sacré-Cœur

*F*rance's capital has been embellished by kings, emperors and presidents, for nine centuries, since the local Celts (the Parisii) first sheltered from Viking and Roman invaders on an island in the Seine (today's Île de la Cité). The result is a strikingly beautiful and memorable city, with a number of delightful, intimate local quarters. The plains of Île-de-France extend far around Paris – castles, cathedrals, churches and picturesque villages are all within one to two hours' drive, often less by train, and are ideal for daytrips or longer excursions.

Paris

Don't miss

Monumental Paris Climb La Défense's Grande Arche for a view of the five mile line-up running east through Napoleon Bonaparte's Arc de Triomphe and place de la Concorde's Egyptian obelisk, to the Louvre pyramid. North of la place de la Concorde, the Grands Boulevards were planned by Napoleon III's Prefect of Paris, Baron Hausmann. In contrast, close by are the exquisitely-enclosed place Vendôme, or the Opéra Garnier.

Notre-Dame

Arc de Triomphe

A trip on the Seine Take a Bateau-bus (quai de Montebello) for a guided tour with unforgettable views.
Île de la Cité Visit Notre-Dame and its fascinating archaeological crypt (place du Parvis), the heavenly Sainte-Chapelle and the Conciergerie dungeons in the nearby Palais de Justice.
Île St-Louis (behind Notre-Dame) Pleasant cafés, quays, quiet streets, tempting small shops, restaurants and hotels.

Montmartre and the Sacré-Cœur basilica (métro Anvers). Place du Tertre is picturesque but touristy – Renoir's Moulin de la Galette is still there and the rickety Bateau Lavoir studios (birthplace of Picasso's *Demoiselles d'Avignon*) have been rebuilt (place Émile-Goudeau). Musée de Montmartre is off rue St-Vincent.

Marais (métro St-Paul or Bastille) a lively, trendy quarter of shops, restaurants and town houses (*hôtels particuliers*). Visit Hôtel Carnavalet, home of 17th-century letter-writer Madame de Sévigné, for its superb interiors.

Macabre Paris Residents of Père-Lachaise cemetery (métro Père-Lachaise) include Jim Morrison, medieval lovers Abelard and Éloïse, Oscar Wilde, Édith Piaf, Sarah Bernhardt and Chopin. Free plans from the kiosk inside the gate. Take an official guided tour of the vast skull-lined catacombs (entrance, place Denfert-Rochereau).

Techno Paris Visit the '19th-century futurist' Eiffel Tower (pure Jules Verne), the spectacular Arts et Métiers métro station (re-vamped in honour of the *Nautilus*), or the Palais de la Découverte science museum. Fine modern buildings include UNESCO's HQ, the Institut du Monde Arabe and the new Grande Bibliothèque Nationale (national library).

The Puces (flea) market, (métro Porte de Clignancourt) – dealers' semi-permanent stands are grouped into specialised sectors.

Parisian art

Le Grand Louvre, uncrowded beyond the famous 'three things worth seeing': *Mona Lisa, Venus de Milo* and *Winged Victory of Samothrace*.

Impressionists and Post Impressionists The Orangerie (Tuileries

Musée d'Orsay

gardens) for Monet's *Waterlilies*; Musée d'Orsay (métro Musée d'Orsay), a stunningly-converted station, with everything from Manet's *Déjeuner sur l'Herbe* to Van Gogh and Cézanne.

Modern Art Musée National d'Art Moderne in the Centre Pompidou (métro Rambuteau) for Picasso, Matisse, Mondrian, Kandinsky (selected works showing until 1999). Georges Braque's studio is reconstructed on the piazza. Also Musée d'Art Moderne de la Ville de Paris (av du Président Wilson).

Other museums Musée du Moyen-Âge (métro Cluny-La Sorbonne) features all things medieval in a beautiful 15th-century mansion; Musée Picasso (métro St-Paul) displays the works Picasso kept for himself; Musée Rodin (métro Varenne) is in Rodin's former town house (*The Kiss, Balzac, The Thinker*).

Cafés and restaurants

Book ahead for the very best restaurants such as Le Pré Catalan in the Bois de Boulogne, or La Tour d'Argent, 15 quai de la Tournelle, ask your hotel to check out deals on Minitel, or stroll around the Marais, Montparnasse and Montmartre for a high density of reasonably-priced local favourites. Reliable recommendations from your hotel or *Pariscope* magazine's *Time Out* section and the French guide *Paris Pas Cher*.

Montparnasse The immortal Left Bank brasseries beloved of Hemingway, Sartre and co: Deux Magots (place St-Germain), La Closerie des Lilas, Brasserie Lipp (171 and 151 boulevard de Montparnasse), Le Sélect (boulevard St-Michel) and La Coupole (102 boulevard de Montparnasse).

Around the Marais Ma Bourgogne (corner of place des Vosges/rue des Francs-Bourgeois), brasserie; Wally le Saharien (16 rue le Regrattier), authentic Saharan specialities, couscous; La Canaille (near place de la Bastille, 4 rue Crillon) and one of the many Île St-Louis eateries, L'Îlot Vache (35 rue St-Louis-en-l'Île).

Montmartre Chez Ginette (101 rue Caulaincourt); L'Auberge Montmartroise (6 rue des Abbesses) and Chartier (7 rue du Faubourg), excellent, cheap pot-au-feu, sumptuous setting, queues.

Passy Au Cadre Vert (4 rue Lekain).

Museums often serve good lunches. Musée d'Orsay has a tearoom with roof terrace and a smart first floor restaurant; Le Grand Louvre restaurant is in the Pyramid basement.

Department store cafés/brasseries include La Samaritaine's stunning roof terrace and Brasserie Flo, beneath Printemps' breathtaking stained glass dome.

Clubs and nightlife
Montmartre's Moulin Rouge (place Blanche) or Folies-Bergères (32 rue Richer) for a nightly knees-up with tourist coachloads.

Marais for smart gay bars and clubs.

Pigalle and Montmartre for dance venues and live music: Divan du Monde (75 rue des Martyrs), hip and historic; Le Bal de l'Élysée-Montmartre (72 boulevard Rochechouart) and The Village (40 rue Fontaine) for over 25s only. Paris's club scene is young and late.

Paris for children
Jardin d'Acclimatation (métro Porte Maillot) features roundabouts, a train-ride, and a mini-zoo. Cité des Enfants playworlds at Parc de la Villette, and Disneyland Paris (RER line A4 direction Marne-la-Vallée).

Paris' transport
The underground Métro and metropolitan train (RER) lines are numbered; look at the terminus shown to check the train's direction. *Paris Visite* tickets (at main métro and RER stations, airports, tourist offices) cover buses, trains and RER

(city centre, both airports, Disney-land Paris) for two, three or five days. For central Paris only, *carnets* of ten tickets (usable on buses and métro trains) are cheaper – from stations and *tabacs* displaying the métro symbol. Métros close about 1 am; Night buses (*Noctambus*) run from place du Châtelet and stops with the owl symbol.

Both Paris's international airports, Orly (south) and Roissy/Charles-de-Gaulle (north-east) are accessible by RER and bus. All the main railway stations; SNCF Gare du Nord – for Eurostar – St-Lazare, Gare de l'Est, Gare de Lyon and Austerlitz have metro connections.

For daytrips from Paris take the RER, SNCF Banlieue or Grandes Lignes. Outside Paris, public transport cross-country is virtually non-existent – longer tours are best by car or bike.

Taxis charge more for extra items in the boot; they won't stop if you hail them too near a taxi rank.

If you're on foot, equip yourself with Michelin's Blue Paris Plan 11 – hundreds of useful addresses and streetfinder maps.

Île-de-France

Don't miss

North of Paris
Royaumont's 13th-century abbey church was ransacked by post-Revolutionary atheists, sparing the cloister, abbot's palace and refectory.
Chantilly castle (N1/N16 north) replaced a Gallo-Roman fort (Cantilius). Visit the Prince de Condé's grand apartments, fine art collections and library (including the *Très Riches Heures du Duc de Berry* and a Gutenberg Bible); also the 18th-century stables – superb dressage displays.

Senlis' Gallo-Roman ramparts (six miles east, D924) enclose a delightful medieval quarter and cathedral.

North-east of Paris
Reims All French monarchs were crowned in the cathedral, now restored and rebuilt after the First World War. Visit eleventh-century St-Rémi basilica, the 17th-century Palais du Tau, and Musée-Hôtel Vergeur (place du Forum) for Dürer engravings. Champagne is the local tipple, invented here by monastic cellar-master Dom Pierre Pérignon. Ask at the tourist information for tours of brand headquarters.

South of Paris
Fontainebleau is dominated by its royal palace, where Napoleon Bonaparte left for exile from the Cour des Adieux. State rooms include the Napoleonic museum and throne-room, plus Marie-Antoinette's tiny mother-of-pearl boudoir and the magnificent chapel, ballroom, library and galleries.

Chartres cathedral

The villages of the Seine valley

Moret-sur-Loing (off N6 south) medieval gateways and watermill; Samois-sur-Seine (D137 north) riverfront villas, restaurants, houseboats, home of Django Rheinhardt; and the chic artists' village of Barbizon (off N7) – visit the Auberge de Ganne museum.

Villages of the Brie D116/115

north to the castles of Blandy-les-Tours and Vaux-le-Vicomte, Champeaux with its 13th-century church and famous 15th-century misericordia, and Rampillon – 13th-century Templar church with elaborate carved west doors.

Chartres, Orléans and the Loire

Feasible in a long weekend. A11 south-west to Chartres's magnificent cathedral; signposted walk in Old Chartres. Take N154/N20 to Orléans's Cathédrale Ste-Croix and 15th-century Maison Jeanne d'Arc; then on to the clearly sign-posted castles of the Loire valley: Chambord, Cheverny (Captain Haddock's castle, in *Tintin* books), Blois, Amboise and Le Clos Lucé (where Leonardo da Vinci ended his days), Chenonceaux and Tours' Old Town and cathedral quarter (place Plumereau). Beyond Tours, Villandry (best in July/August for the ornamental kitchen garden), Langeais, Azay-le-Rideau, Ussé, Chinon and Saumur. Relieve châteaux-fatigue at Doué-la-Fontaine's (D960 south-west of Saumur) remarkable zoo and stay in a local troglodyte house (a so-called *troglogîte*).

West of Paris

St-Cloud, formal gardens of Napoleon's ill-fated Imperial residence.

Rueil-Malmaison, Empress Joséphine's beloved home.

Versailles Louis XIV's incomparably fabulous palace. Everything (royal apartments, Hall of Mirrors, chapel, opera house) is over-the-top. The gardens are a public park incorporating the Grand and Petit Trianon residences, and the 'country village' (*hameau*) where popular legend envisaged Marie-Antoinette playing milk-maid. Details of fountain shows (*grandes eaux*) and nocturnal visits from tourist info but note: the statues are wrapped in winter.

Chambord

Alsace and Lorraine

Strasbourg

*B*ordered by Belgium, Luxembourg, Germany and Switzerland, France's easternmost regions include Lorraine's sombre Great War monuments to the north and Alsace's idyllic vineyards and half-timbered mountain villages, popular with summer walkers and climbers, to the south. Not forgetting distinctive local traditions of art (at Nancy), food, delicious white wines, folklore (see Holidays, p29) and beer!

Strasbourg, once at the heart of Europe's main 'theatre of war', is now a major international city spearheading progress towards European unity (see the Palais de l'Europe, below), with plenty of 'Tyrolean' charm and hospitality to boot.

Strasbourg

Don't miss

Notre-Dame cathedral, featuring a 13th-century carved main doorway, a spectacular spire and twelfth–14th-century windows (the St Christopher is the largest stained-glass figure in the world). Also an astronomical clock with figures of Christ and Death, etc (parade at 12.30pm). Nearby lies France's oldest pharmacy; 16th-century maison Kamerzell.

Place du Château museums (south side of cathedral) Arts Décoratifs (18th-century interiors, Alsatian ceramics), Beaux-Arts (Italian Renaissance, 15th–17th-century Dutch/Flemish paintings) Art Moderne (Impressionists, Gauguin, Klimt) and cathedral treasures.

A stroll through the Old Town taking in Musée Alsacien (folk interiors, costumes), the picturesque 13th-century Cour du Corbeau, and Petite France (down rue des Serruriers) – more a 'Tyrolean Venice' – with its quai de la Petite France and covered bridges.

The Palais de l'Europe (allée de la Robertsau), seat of the European Parliament and Court of Human Rights, lies beyond the centre, opposite the Orangerie park.

Cafés and restaurants

S'burjerstuewel (10 rue des Sangliers) a typical *winstub* (local winebar) noted for regional wines, beers, food and lashings of atmosphere.

Buerehiesel Dine with the Eurocrats at the Orangerie's restored lakeside farmhouse.

The rest of Alsace

Don't miss

Route des Vins and ***Route des
Crêtes*** – detailed touring routes
covering Alsace's best vineyards and
scenery are available from Tourist
Information.
Hohwald region Picturesque
Obernai and Andlau; Alsace's 'holy
mountain' Mont Ste-Odile (annual
pilgrimage 13 December).
Colmar Explore its Old Town;
delightful houses in rue des
Marchands. Superb Musée
d'Unterlinden with Grünewald's
15th-century Issenheim altarpiece;
'Little Venice' quarter (rue du
Manège, rue de la Poissonerie)
with boat trips from pont St-Pierre.
Villages north of Colmar (Turck-
heim, Ammerschwihr, Nieder-
mohrschwir etc N415/D35) are
pure Alsace (some have rooftop
storks' nests). Also Haut Koenigs-
bourg castle.

Gérardmer (west of Colmar) gracious
'lakes-and-mountains' summer/ski
resort in Parc Naturel Régional des
Ballons des Vosges. Superb panorama from Le Hohneck. Good
walking (footpath GR5), skiing and
climbing from the villages around
the four Ballons summits.
Mulhouse (south of Colmar)
pronounced 'moo-looze'. Stroll
through its historic quarter (from
place de la Réunion) and its *Nouveau
Quartier* (between place de la
République and the Rhône/Rhine
canal). Good national transport
museums and, nearby, the
Écomusée d'Alsace featuring 60
restored traditional buildings and
working craftshops.
The Franche-Comté (A36 south-
west from Mulhouse) is a longer
drive but worth it for the glorious
rural countryside. Le Corbusier's
chapel Notre-Dame-du-Haut (N19
between Belfort and Lure) is all the
more remarkable.

Nancy

Don't miss

Place Stanislas, a beautiful 18th-
century square. The Musée des
Beaux-Arts has excellent collections
of paintings and glassware.
Palais Ducal, magnificently rebuilt
and restored, housing the Musée
Historique Lorrain (regional
archaeology and history, luminously
spiritual paintings of Georges de
La Tour).
Art Nouveau architecture France's
Arts and Crafts movement
galvanised the region's traditional
crystal, glass and furniture industries.
Visit the Excelsior brasserie (3 rue
Mazagran), decorated by glass
designer and manufacturer Louis
Majorelle (1 rue Louis-Majorelle).

Colmar

Also Musée de l'École de Nancy (rue Sergent-Blandan), a period townhouse with Art Nouveau interiors.

The rest of Lorraine

Don't miss

Metz Visit Cathédrale St-Étienne, known as 'God's lantern' for its wonderful 13th–16th-century stained glass, including a Chagall window; see also the Cour d'Or museum (rue des Jardins) for superbly-presented local archaeological remains, fine arts (Delacroix, Corot) and arms.

Verdun (west of Metz) Visit the *Ville Haute* and the fortified citadel by Louis XIV's celebrated military architect Vauban. Visitors can explore the citadel's four and a half miles of subterranean vaulted passages (where off-duty World War

One soldiers were billeted), and the battlefield's monuments and war cemeteries nearby.

The Maginot Line, France's 'impregnable' defences, between the Meuse and the Rhine. Various sites, including Hackenberg and Simershof, are visitable.

Domrémy-la-Pucelle Tiny birthplace of Joan of Arc. Joan-abilia abounds. The parish church has a twelfth-century baptismal font.

Petits trains touristiques scenic trains run from Volgelsheim and Breisach along the Rhine (east of Colmar), and also near Cernay, east of Thann.

Alsace and Lorraine's transport
Strasbourg is the main international airport, or take the Paris–Strasbourg train(via Nancy or Belfort/Mulhouse) in about four hours. A car or bike is best for exploring but cyclists may find southern Alsace's mountain roads punishing.

Eguisheim

Lyon and the surrounding countryside

*C*ommanding the confluence of the mighty Rhône and Saône, France's ancient Gallo-Roman capital offers antique ruins and atmospheric medieval and Renaissance quarters. It's also an ideal starting point from which to explore the peaceful villages and vineyards of Burgundy (Bourgogne, to the north), France's top Alpine ski resorts (also popular with summer walkers and climbers), and the remote, rural, idyllic Auvergne (west); not forgetting the Rhône valley's world-famous vineyards (AOC Côtes du Rhône) to the south.

Lyon

Don't miss

Old Lyon Take time to explore the Renaissance St-Jean quarter (over the Sâone, by footbridge from place Bellecour), criss-crossed by 'secret' passageways (*traboules*) often hidden behind massive doors and much-used by the World War Two Resistance. Ask for a map at Bellecour's Tourist Information; look out for the spiral staircase at 10 rue de Lainerie or the elegant cour de Philibert de l'Orme at 8 rue de la Juiverie.

Croix-Rousse district Steep streets and steps lead from place Sathonay to boulevard de la Croix-Rousse and its Monday to Saturday morning market (or take the number 6 trolley-bus from place des Terreaux). Fine views from the *gros caillou*, a glacial boulder mounted at the eastern end (excellent Café du Gros Caillou nearby). A famous *traboule* known as the Cour des Voraces runs down from 9 place Colbert to 29 rue Imbert Colomès.

Fourvière and Gallo-Roman Lyon Funiculars climb from avenue du Doyenné, one to Fourvière's 19th-century Byzantine basilica, the other (*funiculaire St-Just*) to the ancient amphitheatres and Musée de la Civilisation Gallo-Romaine (fine mosaics, statuary).

Musée des Beaux Arts (place des Terreaux) fine 18th- and 19th-century paintings in a former abbey.

Institut Lumière (25 rue du Premier-

Saint Nizier church, Lyon

Annecy

Film) cinema history in the Lumière brothers' family château.
Musée des Tissus (34 rue de la Charité) sumptuous textiles in an 18th-century town house.

Cafés and restaurants

Peninsular Lyon The central restaurant quarter is rue Mercière and rue des Marroniers. Try Chez Perret (métro Bellecour), Café des Négociants (2 place Francisque-Régaud) and gastronome Paul Bocuse's twin brasseries, Le Nord (11 place Antonin Ponçet) and Le Sud (18 rue Neuve). La Mère Vittet (near Perrache métro/train station) opens round-the-clock, every day.
In Old Lyon don't miss a traditional *bouchon* (brasserie). Try Le Vieux Lyon (44 rue St-Jean), La Tablée du Gône (place du Petit-Collège), Chez Chabert (14 quai Romain-Rolland).

Lyon for children

Guignol, France's Mr Punch is from Lyon. Shows are at 2 rue Louis Carrand (métro Vieux Lyon).
Parc de la Tête d'Or (métro Masséna) features a pleasant free zoo, carousels and playgrounds.
Palais de la Miniature (2 rue de la Juiverie) presents amazing scaled-down replicas – everything from a Lyon café to a modern warehouse.

Lyon's transport

Satolas international airport is a long way out – take the shuttle service. The main rail terminus is Lyon Part-Dieu. Explore on foot; use the métro in a hurry. City and métro maps, bus timetables etc: from tourist information at Part-Dieu and Perrache stations, place Bellecour (métro Bellecour).

Daytrips from Lyon

Musée Mémorial des Enfants d'Izieu (exit Chimlin/Les Abrets, D592) commemorates Jewish children hidden here and deported in 1944 (the subject of the film *Au Revoir les Enfants*).
Mâcon and Côtes du Rhône wine regions, north and south on the N6 and N86 respectively. Visit the remains of the tenth-century abbey of Cluny, near Mâcon (N6 north, N79, D980).
An excursion into the Auvergne Drive west to Clermont-Ferrand and the famous *puys*, extinct volcanoes with spectacular cone craters (Puy de Dôme, de Mary, de Sancy). From St-Étienne (south-west), explore Allier and the Cantal.
Gastronomic meccas Paul Bocuse at Collonges on the Sâone (04 72 42 90 90) and Les Trois Gros at Roanne (04 77 71 66 97).

Mont-Blanc

Côte d'Azur

casino, Monte-Carlo

*T*he winding corniche roads and remote dead-end valleys of the Côte d'Azur's mountainous hinterland can be a navigator's nightmare – but persevere! Some of France's wildest landscapes, most picturesque hill-villages, finest art and best skiing are all within two hours drive of the seafront splendours of Nice or Cannes. There's no fooling the jet set . . .

Nice

Don't miss

The seafront promenade des Anglais subsidized by Nice's already sizeable British colony in 1820, featuring the splendiferous 1906 Hôtel Négresco (corner of rue de Rivoli). Quai des États-Unis sweeps on around Baie des Anges.
Old Nice From cours Saleya climb to place St-François. Palais Lascaris features sumptuous interiors and tapestries. Superb views from the castle headland.
Cimiez, for Musée Matisse, Gallo-Roman remains, and a Franciscan monastery (av des Arènes-de-Cimiez). Musée Chagall (the world's largest collection) is in a lovely park (av du Dr-Ménard).
More museums Choose from Beaux-Arts Jules Chéret (av des Baumettes) – Italian primitives, 19th-century painting; Masséna (near the Négresco); Raoul Dufy (quai des États-Unis) for charming local views, and Art Moderne et Contemporain (boulevard Risso), a stunning building housing works by the likes of Picasso and Oldenburg.

Cafés and restaurants
Old Nice and cours Saleya Lively cafés and bars.
Nissa Socca (rue Ste-Réparate) Italianate Niçois specialities including socca bread made with chick-pea flour.
Grand Café Turin (place Garibaldi) Seafood/oyster bar, evenings only in winter.

Carlton plage, Cannes

Cannes

Don't miss

La Croisette seafront First stop: palais des Festivals (1982) and its famous steps, centrepiece of Cannes' May film festival. Nearby, allée des Stars features famous handprints. At the super-glitzy eastern end: window-shopping and star-spotting on the private board-walks of the various grand hotels.

Le Suquet Old Cannes, on the headland overlooking the port. The eleventh-century castle holds Musée de la Castre and has an impressive watch-tower (superb panorama).

A boat trip from the port to the Iles de Lérins Ste-Marguerite has shady forests and the eighteenth-century Fort Royal prison. Cleaner water and a pleasant walk on the sea-facing side of St-Honorat.

Cafés and restaurants

Reasonably-priced local favourites are found around the port at the west end of La Croisette and Le Suquet.

Beach front stands (boulevard Jean Hibert) serve *pan-bagna* and hot merguez sandwiches, chips etc.

Beach cafés have private terraces with sun-loungers and parasols for rent, and often ping-pong tables and pin-ball too.

Le Boucanier, west at La Napoule (port Mandelieu), overlooks the marina, beach and castle.

Biot, the nearby hill village. Look out for Les Arcades (superb food and stylish 15th-century rooms) and Café Brun, a hip Dutch pub serving delicious beers and Indonesian food.

Monte-Carlo

The coast and *l'arrière-pays*

Don't miss

A drive along the coast roads

Glorious views and colourful towns; explore at leisure from St-Tropez to Monte-Carlo.

■ 'St-Trop' mixes Provençal charm and jet-set glitz (the port, La Ponche, place des Lices) see also Musée de l'Annonciade (Signac, Matisse, Cross, Dufy, Bonnard).

■ Take the coast path around Baie des Canebiers/Cap de St-Tropez for quiet (often naturist) beaches and inlets. The N98 (or the equally spectacular Pic du Cap Roux forest road from Agay) leads on to Cannes.

■ Antibes offers Château Grimaldi: ceramics and installations by Picasso.

■ Further east, Cap Ferrat features the Rothschild-Ephrussi and Villa Kerylos mansions. Monaco's old quarter: the Royal palace, and the cathedral where Rainier III married Grace Kelly, on the craggy Rocher peninsula.

A tour inland from Cannes

■ At Vallauris, the castle museum features Picasso's *Guerre et Paix* fresco and ceramics.

■ Mougins – Picasso's home before his death – has a fine panorama from the clock-tower (key from photography museum, opposite).

■ Stop for a drink in Valbonne's pleasant, café-lined, arcaded central square.

■ Gourdon's castle, dizzily perched above Gorges du Loup, houses a remarkable private collection of paintings, arms etc.

■ Follow D3/D6 through the gorge to D2210 (direction Tourettes-sur-Loup) and the ancient town of Vence: excellent historic walk signposted from place du Frêne, also Matisse's Chapelle du Rosaire.

■ Wind back to Cannes via St-Paul and the Fondation Maeght (modern art), Roquefort-les-Pins and Biot (Musée National Fernand Léger, famous glassworks, good restaurants).

St-Tropez

St-Paul-de-Vence

A drive through Nice's hinterland
Wild, dead-end mountain valleys
and winding roads.
■ D19 north to Gorges de la
Vésubie, then left (D32) to Utelle
(St-Véran church) and the sanctuary
and panorama of Madone d'Utelle.
■ Back on D2565 to St-Martin-
Vésubie and the remote Parc
National du Mercantour (maps
from Bureau des Guides in Tende,
04 93 04 73 71).
■ D94 leads on to Vallon de la
Madone de Fenestre, popular with
summer climbers.
■ For Mercantour's east side, take
D2564 from Nice to the village of
Roquebrune, then follow Sospel and
N204 to Breil-sur-Roya, Saorge and
Tende. Summer guided hikes from
Casterino to the Vallée des
Merveilles (prehistoric rock-
carvings).
Skiing
Isola 2000 A straight run from
Nice; also Barcelonette, Sauze
and Super-Sauze are about two
hours away.
Transport on the Côte d'Azur
Nice international airport serves the
whole coast: take the shuttle bus
(*la navette*) to Nice's bus station
(promenade Paillon) or the Métrazur
(frequent rail links between all Côte
d'Azur towns) from St-Augustin
station nearby or Nice's main rail
terminus (Avenue Thiers). Cannes'
train station is on rue Jean-Jaurès;

the bus station is in front of the
Hôtel de Ville. Some day trips are
possible by bus but you'll need a car
for touring.

Côte d'Azur for children
Away from the tempting but
crowded beaches, try Fréjus safari
park or Marineland (between
Antibes and Biot; dolphins etc).
In Monaco, visit the Musée
Océanographique's amazing
aquarium, the doll and puppet
museum (Musée des Poupées et
Automates) or the Observatoire
cave. The Nice-to-Annot train,
Train des Pignes, is steam for the
last stretch (Puget–Theniers):
May–September only.

St-Paul-de-Vence

Provence and Languedoc

Pont du Gard

*F*rance's hottest, driest regions feature Roman cities, ancient villages rich in folklore (see Holidays, p29), and a varied coastline of sandy beaches, crystalline cliffs and lively ports.

Aix-en-Provence and Marseille are 25 minutes and several worlds apart – a medieval university town of mellow facades, shaded squares and fountains, and a brash and vibrant port whose street-life and markets reflect significant Algerian, Vietnamese, West-African, Caribbean, Comorran (Indian Ocean) and Armenian communities, plus Foreign Legionnaires and sailors!

Further inland, the bright light, heat and (sometimes) scouring winds of the northern hills may discourage cyclists; take your car (and the occasional walk or horse ride) to savour the enchanting sights, scents and sounds – spectacular gorges, lavender fields, wild herbs and Provence's 'singing bug', the cicada.

Aix-en-Provence

Don't miss

Cours Mirabeau Aix's famous promenade, lined with 17th-century *hôtels* (town houses), cafés, plane trees and fountains – a thermal spring feeds the middle one, which steams in winter.

Quartier Mazarin a mid-17th-century grid of streets with fine *hôtels*, the Fontaine des Quatre Dauphins, and the 13th-century Gothic St-Jean-de-Malte whose priory houses Musée Granet (local archaeology, European old masters, small Cézanne gallery).

A stroll through old Aix taking in the 16th-century Tour de l'Horloge with its Provençal wrought-iron work and animated clock, and Cathédrale St-Sauveur, whose ancient baptistry incorporates Roman columns.

the Rotunda, Aix-en-Provence

Paul Cézanne's house, designed by him in 1897. Cézanne immortalised *le pays d'Aix* but was unbeloved of its bourgeoisie, hence his low-key presence among the bequests displayed at Musée Granet. The studio (9 av Paul-Cézanne) is unchanged since his death.

Saturday morning market (place de Verdun) for fresh produce,

18

antiques, kelims, Provençal ceramics, textiles and soaps.

Cafés and restaurants
Café des Deux Garçons (near passage Agard) Cours Mirabeau's first café (in every sense). Ornate interior, but the terrace is best. Excellent lunch staples and specials.
Place des Cardeurs is lively on summer nights. L'Hacienda (south-east corner) serves good, inexpensive menus in a pretty side square.

Marseille

Don't miss

The Vieux Port (métro Vieux Port Hôtel de Ville) Yachts bob where Phocaean Greek traders from Asia-Minor landed, in around 600BC, to found Massilia. See the Greek ramparts and a freeze-dried Roman ship at Jardin des Vestiges/ Musée d'Histoire de Marseille (rue H. Barbusse); also Musée des Docks Romains (place Vivaux).
Basilique St-Victor, the port's fortress/abbey (south side), built over a third-century shrine, fifth-century crypt and catacombs dedicated to Lazarus and Mary Magdalene.
The Panier A picturesque quarter on the port's north side. Take Montée des Accoules to the restored Vieille Charité poor-house, now home to museums of Mediterranean archaeology and African, Oceanian and Amerindian art.
More museums Beaux-Arts and Histoire Naturelle (Natural History) in the grandiose palais Longchamp (métro Longchamp Cinq Avenues), Cantini (métro Estrangin-Préfecture) for modern art – Miro, Bacon, Arp, Max Ernst and the Surrealists.
Vallon des Auffes, picturesque port and gourmet Mecca, south of the Vieux Port (corniche Président

Kennedy). Chez Fonfon serves a famously good, authentic *bouillabaisse* (see p73).
La Cité Radieuse (boulevard Michelet) Pleasant third-floor hotel and restaurant in Le Corbusier's revolutionary 1945 stilt-building.
A boat-trip from quai des Belges to Marseille's islands Frioule features deserted creeks, fragrant *maquis* (wild thyme, rosemary) and restaurants; Château d'If was the fictional prison of Dumas' Count of Monte-Cristo.

Transport in Aix and Marseille
Buses run from Marseille Marignane international airport to St-Charles central rail terminus and Aix's coach terminus. Coaches run every 15 minutes between Marseille (place Victor Hugo, next to St-Charles) and Aix (rue Lapierre, behind main post office, west of the cours Mirabeau). Stroll around Marseille's Vieux Port area, otherwise take the bus (quai des Belges, back of the Vieux Port) or métro. Tickets, from stations or *bar-tabacs*, are interchangeable between buses and the métro under certain conditions – double check! Aix is delightful on foot, nightmarish by car.

vieux port, Marseille

the Camargue

Exploring Provence

Don't miss

The Lubéron Visit Bonnieux and neighbouring villages Lacoste, Ménerbes, Saignon, also Roussillon's nearby ochre workings. Drive on to Gordes (stop for a drink at the Cercle Républicain), the Cistercian abbey of Sénanque and the dry-stone Village des Bories. Mysterious Fontaine-de-Vaucluse (west, nearby) is the world's deepest water-filled chasm. From the watermills of l'Isle-sur-la-Sorgue, follow Cavaillon/N7 or A7 back to Aix/Marseille. There are fine walks on footpath GR9/97; the Gorges de Regalon (off D973 west of Mérindol) are a short, scenic scramble.

Avignon hosted the papacy from 1309 through the Great Schism until 1417, hence the breathtaking Palais des Papes. Restaurants cover nearby place de l'Horloge. The famous un-finished bridge (Pont St-Bénézet) is on boulevard de la Ligne. Nearby the Roman city of Orange and Mont Ventoux (superb panorama and good skiing) are also worth a visit.

Les Baux-de-Provence and Arles North to Sénas, and on through the Alpilles hills to Les Baux, a half-deserted village perched on a spectacular crag. Close by are St-Rémy (impressive Roman remains) and the entrance to the Rhône delta, with fortifications at Beaucaire and Tarascon. In Arles, don't miss St-Trophime's Romanesque cloister, the Roman arena and theatre, Constantine's palace and the ancient Alyscamps cemetery. Restaurant terraces fill the central place du Forum.

The Camargue Les Saintes-Maries-de-la-Mer has good beaches and restaurants. The church tower gives superb views of surrounding salt marshes which are best explored off-piste with an organised 4x4 safari (from regional tourist offices). Mountain-bikers, hikers or fearless drivers could try the unmade track from Faraman, near Salin-de-Giraud, to Beauduc; never stray off the dykes. From Salin take the Bac de Barcarin car ferry across the Rhône to the Marseille road.

Eastern Provence From Aix, D17 east to Le Tholonet below 'Cézanne's mountain', the Sainte-Victoire (park and walk to the Barrage Zola at Bibémus; summit hike from Vauvenargues on D10, north). D23/D952 north-east to Moustiers and the Grand Canyon du Verdon (hike through it in a day on the punishing GR4 path from

Bonnieux

La-Palud-sur-Verdon). D955 south to Draguignan, then west through quiet countryside and villages (Tourtour, Sillans-la-Cascade) to the Cistercian abbey of Thoronet. West again, to St-Maximin (13th-century basilica, fine crypt sarcophagi) and the Sainte-Baume massif. From here, D2/D80 west to Aubagne, Aix and Marseille.

The Provençal coast The N568/D5 leads west from Marseille towards the Camargue along the hills of l'Estaque (picturesque inlets at Niolon, Madrague-de-Gignac). East of Marseille, take D559 to Cassis. From the harbour, explore the white cliffs and sapphire waters of the Calanques (Port-Miou, Port-Pin, En-Vau) by boat or on the slithery GR98 footpath. Good beaches and islands around Toulon/Hyères. Inland, explore the wild forests of the Massif des Maures.

Languedoc

Don't miss

Montpellier Esplanade Charles-de-Gaulle is a typical Languedoc *ramblas* (promenade) flanking the hi-tech/post-modern Polygone and Antigone quarters (across Jardin du Champ de Mars). The smartly restored Old Town leads up to panoramic Promenade du Peyrou, built in 1688 to welcome the St-Clément aqueduct. Montpellier's *folies* (castles) are a short drive, at Château d'O, Flaugergues and la Mogère.

The Hérault and the Cévennes Take the D986 north through St-Martin-de-Londres and Ganges to the Cévennes National Park. Take D9 from Florac to Anduze, then D982 back to Ganges (spectacular caves at the Grotte des Demoiselles); D4 to St-Guilhem-le-Désert (eleventh-century abbey and cloister; Grotte de la Clamouse) and the Gorges de l'Hérault.

The Languedoc coast Explore from Cap d'Agde (twelfth-century basalt Cathédrale St-Étienne and self-contained naturist village) to La Grande Motte's ziggurat apartments (N112/ D62). The colourful port of Sète has a great market (Wednesday and Friday mornings), a fascinating mariners' cemetery and singer-songwriter Georges Brassens' birth-place (Espace Brassens). Nearby, sample Frontignan's muscat wine; Palavas-les-Flots offers sweeping beaches.

Roman Languedoc, a short hop north-east of La Grande Motte. Nîmes features the Maison Carrée (the world's best-preserved Roman temple) and the famous Arènes (amphitheatre), centre of the annual *feria* (see p29). The Pont du Gard aqueduct (off N86, north-east) has straddled the Gardon valley since 19BC, its top level some 130ft up (you can walk across, but there are no barriers). The A9 motorway follows the route of the Roman Via Domitia.

South-west France

la place de la Bourse, Bordeaux

*B*ordered to the south by the snow-capped Pyrenees, south-west France includes the tranquil Dordogne and Lot valleys, plus the best of both kinds of beach: l'océan *(the Atlantic)* and la mer méditerranée *(the Mediterranean)*. There are splendid medieval castles and cities, mountain spas and fine vineyards *(hearty reds from Bordeaux, Bergerac, Cahors, Corbières; intense sweet whites from Banyuls)*, all easily explored by car from Bordeaux and Toulouse.

Bordeaux is a wealthy river port, not large, but imposing thanks to the grandiose plans of the 18th-century Intendants *(local 'regents')*. Huge civic buildings and gateways line the Garonne's west bank; broad boulevards sweep past the grand theatre *(place de la Comédie)*.

Toulouse, in contrast, is a brick-built medieval gem – a colourful, exuberant, distinctly southern university city with world-class art collections, which remains relatively *(inexplicably)* unscathed by tourism.

Bordeaux

Don't miss

Port Cailhau, Bordeaux

Old Bordeaux (quartier de la Rouselle), untouched by the Intendants. Explore from place Bir Hakeim on the waterfront.
Place du Parlement 18th-century Bordeaux, with Louis-XV arcades sheltering cafés and restaurants.
Quartier des Chartrons features the *hôtels particuliers* (town houses) of Bordeaux's bourgeois merchant families, and the Musée d'Art Contemporain, strikingly housed in an old wine warehouse.
Other museums Musée d'Aquitaine (regional history), Musée des Beaux-Arts (fine arts, old masters, touring shows) and Musée Jean Moulin (Resistance history).

Window-shopping on the grand boulevards where the local vinocrats buy their antiques, jewellery and international luxury goods.

Cafés, bars and restaurants

Place du Parlement for most tastes and pockets (including seafood, crêpes).

Café les Quatre Sœurs, (next to the theatre) ornate period decor, home-made pastries and pleasant hotel rooms.

Restaurant le Cellier Bordelais (30 quai de la Monnaie) serves fine Bordeaux and good, reasonably-priced food.

Transport in Bordeaux

Mérignac international airport has a shuttle (*navette*) connection into town. Gare St-Jean is the main rail terminus, cours de la Marne. Easily explored on foot, central Bordeaux is also well-served by buses (termini on the waterfront, quai Louis XVIII).

Around Bordeaux

Tour the wine region of Médoc Château Mouton-Rothschild, Château Margaux and Château Lafite.

Dordogne and the Lot Savour the rural peace at leisure! Take D936 to Bergerac, and the back roads to the spectacular cliff village of Rocamadour. The cave-paintings of Lascaux are close by. Kids will enjoy floating through the caverns of the Gouffre de Padirac. Go on to Figeac and follow the beautiful valleys of the

Rocamadour, Lot

Lot or the Célé to Cahors (more delicious AOC wine and a good Sunday morning market). On, down the Lot to Villeneuve-sur-Lot, then Agen for the A62 back to Bordeaux.

St-Émilion is an idyllic medieval stop-over (fine restaurants, cafés, country hotels). The bell-tower (key from tourist office, opposite) provides a panorama of the 200-plus local vineyards. Ask about visitable cellars, tours of the catacombs and the *train des Grands Vignobles* which tours vineyards from the Collégiale.

Watersport lovers head south-west for the Landes' Atlantic beaches, pines and dunes at Biscarosse-Plage and Mimizan-Plage.

Loubressac, Lot

Toulouse

Don't miss

Basilique de St-Sernin, with its ornate Romanesque carvings, crypt and numerous holy relics.

The Jacobins church and convent featuring the relics of St-Thomas Aquinas, and the famous 'palm-tree' pillar.

The Capitole (town hall), seat of the powerful *capitouls* (city consuls) whose turreted town houses dot Old Toulouse. Behind the delightful 18th-century façade, the first-floor Salle des Illustres and adjoining rooms feature vivid 19th-century murals.

A stroll through Old Toulouse (rue St-Rome, rue des Changes, rue de la Bourse . . .). The magnificently-restored Hôtel d'Assezat (rue de Metz) houses the superb Bemberg Collection (fine paintings).

Musée des Augustins (rue de Metz) everything from paleo-Christian sarcophagi to religious paintings (Perugino, Rubens); marvellous romanesque sculpture including pillar capitals from St-Sernin.

A walk or cycle along the Canal du Midi, which flows from Toulouse across Languedoc. Several barge restaurants.

Albi

Cafés and restaurants

L'Assiette à l'Oie and **La Réserve** (both on rue Peyrolières) Both have excellent value lunch menus (local specialities). La Réserve also serves local game (trout, venison, boar).

Bistrot Van Gogh (place St-Georges) Sunny terrace, atmospheric interior occasional live jazz.

Le Sherpa (rue du Taur) Popular café (salads, crêpes, exotic teas).

Marché Victor-Hugo (place Victor Hugo) Lively covered market (despite grim building); excellent first-floor eateries.

Transport in Toulouse

Bus number 70 runs into town from Blagnac international airport. The brand-new one-line métro connects Mirail university and the main rail terminus (Matabiau) to the centre, best explored on foot.

Bruniquel, Tarn

round Toulouse

astle-hop with the Albigensian
rusaders (see below): Foix,
Montségur, Peyrepertuse and
Quéribus are all worth visiting.
Thread north from Quéribus
hrough the Corbières (good AOC
vine), or travel along the Aude to the
ortified citadel of Carcassonne.
Hotels and restaurants include Hôtel
u Donjon and the excellent
Auberge de Dame Careas.

Albi another brick masterpiece and
n important base for local Cathar
eretics (hence the 'Albigensian'
rusade of 1209). Albi's Cathédrale
te-Cécile reasserted Catholic power
fter the Cathars' fatal last stand
t Montségur. Hôtel Bosc (rue
Toulouse-Lautrec) is the artist's
irthplace. The Musée Toulouse-
Lautrec houses the family's superb
ollection of his works.

Andorra for tax-free shopping and
Spanish restaurants, good skiing and
ummer trekking. Visit the quiet
Pyrenean villages on N4 and N3.

The Basque country for a change
f architecture, culture, food, even
anguage. Superb beaches (Biarritz)
nd scenery. The shrine of Lourdes
s south of A64 near Tarbes.

French Catalonia (A61/A9 to
Perpignan), for attractive ports
nd beaches (Banyuls, Collioure,
Argelès-Plage, St-Cyprien), remote
mountain abbeys (St-Martin-du-
Canigou; Serrabone) and Pyrenean
cenery – take the little yellow train
e Canari) from Villefranche-de-
Conflent to Latour-de-Carol.

The Lauragais, made wealthy by
he 16th-century trade in blue
astel dyes, is a quiet stretch of
ountry, dotted with attractive
illages and pastel-merchants'
rand country houses. East of here,
rive up into the Montagne Noire
nd the Parc Régional du Haut-
anguedoc.

Lombez, Garonne

Walking in the Pyrenees good
trekking around Andorra on GR7,
and several mountain hikes in the
Basques – GRs 10 and 65.

Laruns, Pyrénées Atlantiques

Brittany and Normandy

Brittany and Normandy are easily reached both from France's 'back door' (the Channel ports of Le Havre, Cherbourg, St-Malo, Roscoff) and Paris. Travel by car or bike, exploring Normandy's deep, shady lanes and half-timbered manors, or Brittany's wild cliffs, beaches, fishing ports and mysterious stone-age monuments. From Nantes, leisured travellers can head south to La Rochelle, Bordeaux and Toulouse, or follow the Loire back to Paris.

Normandy

Don't miss

Monet's haunts Etretat cliffs, Rouen cathedral and its idyllic studio and water-garden at Giverny (N15 Rouen to Vernon, D5 east).
Honfleur Galleries and *crêperies* around the picturesque Vieux Bassin. Close by are super-chic **Trouville** and **Deauville** (vast beaches), and delightful manors at Canapville and Crèvecœur (inland).
The Calvados bocage An ancient (almost unnavigable) landscape of sunken lanes enclosing patchwork fields, extending south and west to Mont-St-Michel, used to advantage

by the World War Two Resistance and Allies.
Caen The castle's Beaux-Arts museum features Rembrandt, Veronese, Rubens. Also 'his and hers' abbeys built by William the Conqueror and his wife Matilde, and the memorial honouring the D-Day landings on nearby Sword, Juno, Gold, Omaha and Utah beaches (war cemeteries and monuments).
Bayeux's famous tapestry (N13 north-west of Caen) recounts another victorious landing, across the Channel in England – that of William the Conqueror in 1066.
Mont-St-Michel's unforgettable silhouette commands the mouth of the river Couesnon, former frontier between the duchies of Normandy and Brittany. Visit the Gothic abbey, early Christian crypt and spectacular 'Merveille' buildings. Avoid the crowds with an overnight stay: Le Mouton Blanc (02 33 60 14 30). Children enjoy the Sirène de la Baie, an amphibious tractor touring the oyster beds from Le Vivier-sur-Mer. Fougères' fairy-tale castle and walled town are a worthwhile inland detour.

le Mont-St-Michel

Brittany

Don't miss

St-Malo St-Malo's twelfth-century sea ramparts and 15th–17th-century castle enclose the Old Town's elegant 'English Georgian' terraces, opposite the ferry-port.

Rennes offers a pleasant old quarter, plus the Musée de Bretagne (Breton history, archaeology and daily life) and excellent Écomusée (rural skills, tools and costumes).

The north Brittany coast, west from Dinard: Tréguier's 14th-century Cathédrale St-Tugdual, Lannion's Old Town and eleventh-century Templar church, plus castles and chapels inland off D11 (Kerfons, Tonquédec, Kergrist). Also Morlaix, the Barnenez tumulus, St-Pol-de-Léon's Kreisker chapel and the basilica of Folgoët (Pardon festival, first Sunday in September).

North Finistère Atlantic cliffs at the beautiful pointe de Penhir (south of Brest) and pointe du Raz (France's much-trampled westernmost point, now being re-planted). Village churches east of Brest feature superb *enclos paroissiaux* (churchyards with elaborate carved gateways and Calvary scenes): visit Landernau Pencran), Lampaul-Guimiliau, Guimiliau and St-Thégennec.

South Finistère and Cornouaille Roman Polanski's *Tess* was partly filmed at the Renaissance village of Locronan. Visit the spectacular Eckmuhl lighthouse and the lonely

church of Notre-Dame de Tronoën (another superb Calvary). Some older ladies still wear the tall local headdress of starched lace. Cornouaille's capital, Quimper, features the Musée de la Faïence (charming local porcelain).

The south Brittany coast At Le Guilvinec, fishing-boats land the day's catch (late afternoon) at the *Criée* (fish-market). On D44 east, the quiet inlet of Ste-Marine (waterfront restaurants and bar/cafés) faces Bénodet across the Odet estuary (boat trips). Good beaches nearby include Beg-Meil and Cap Coz. Concarneau features an island Old Town (rampart walks, crêperies and restaurants), a lively *criée* and boat-trips to the Îles de Glénan. On D783 east, take a riverside walk at Gauguin's old haunt Pont-Aven.

Ancient Brittany: around the Golfe du Morbihan Take a boat trip from the Quiberon peninsula to aptly-named Belle-Île. At the peninsula's land end, Carnac's standing stones march cross-country along D196. Don't miss Musée de la Préhistoire in Carnac village, and nearby St-Michel tumulus (a huge excavated burial mound) off D781 east of Carnac. Locmariaquer (D781/D28 east) features another remarkable group of megaliths. Continue around the beautiful Golfe du Morbihan, a valley in neolithic times, now flooded by the sea. From Larmor Baden take a short boat-trip to the tiny Île de Gavrinis, site of one of Europe's finest neolithic burial chambers.

Holidays, festivals and events

Rouen

There's a heady mixture of high culture, glamourous sporting events and traditional religious holidays. Most large towns organise excellent theatre, film, art or music festivals throughout the year – ask at local tourist offices. *Fêtes patronales* are local patron saint's days, often with parades in traditional costume (eg Brittany's famous parish *Pardons*), fireworks, fairs etc. Bonfires mark the summer solstice and Feast of St John the Baptist (*les feux de la St-Jean*) all over France (June 21–24) and the Assumption of the Virgin/harvest festival (15 August) is a major national holiday. Regional foods and wine are celebrated, too, often by ancient and solemn *confrèries* (guilds) of local producers. France's National Day (July 14, commemorating the 1789 Revolution) is marked with huge firework displays everywhere, and a massive military parade in Paris.

Northern France

Paris, Parc des Princes, Five Nations rugby internationals (January–March).

Cassel (Calais region) Parade of the giants Reuze Maman and Reuze Papa (Easter Monday).
Paris Café waiters' foot race, complete with white aprons and loaded trays! (late May/June).
Paris, Roland Garros stadium French Open tennis championships, on clay. Very glamourous (late May/early June).
Loire castles *Son et lumière* spectaculars, enchanting nocturnal walks (May–September – ask at local tourist offices).
Orléans, Rouen and Reims *Les fêtes Joanniques*, following Joan of Arc's progress to coronation in Reims cathedral (early and late May, early June respectively).
Le Mans 24-hour motor race (June).
Plougastel, Finistère, Brittany Strawberry festival (second Sunday in June).
Samois-sur-Seine Django Reinhardt jazz festival with late-night gipsy street music (late June).
Paris Start and finish of the Tour de France cycle race (July).
Guingamp, Brittany Notre-Dame de Bon Secours, nocturnal parade of the Black Virgin, with bonfire (first weekend in July).
Guînes (near Calais) The *Fête du Camp du Drap d'Or* (Field of the Cloth of Gold) recreates the summit meeting of England's Henry VIII and France's François I in 1520 (mid-July).
Versailles, Paris Summer music in the château gardens (01 39 49 48 24)
Lorient, Brittany *Festival Interceltique* Celtic dance, music and games (first fortnight in August).
Mont-St-Michel Feast of the Archangel Michael (late Sepember).
Paris, Longchamp France's premier horserace, the Prix de l'Arc de Triomphe (October).

Obernai, Bas Rhin

Les Sables d'Olonne (near Nantes)
Start of the famous Vendée Globe
round-the-world single-handed
yacht race (November).

Central France

Mâcon region Winter wine festival
(late January) Free tastings.
Bourges, northern Massif Central
Le Printemps de Bourges, rock and
world music (late spring).
Pont de Cervières, near Briançon
(Alps) Bachu Ber sword dance
15 August).
Lyon hills Accordion music (the
sound of France!) at *Rencontres
Internationales d'Accordéons* (end
October).
Beaune, Burgundy Wine auction of
the Hospices de Beaune (early
November).

Southern and
south-west France

Monte-Carlo road rally (end of
January).
Roquebrune *Fête du Mimosa* (flower
festival) (February).
Nice *Carnaval* features a spectacular
float procession and a huge bonfire
on Mardi Gras night.
Nîmes, Arles and Béziers *Ferias:* bull-
fight festivals (mid-May, Easter
weekend, mid-August respectively)
Cannes International film festival –
spot the stars (late May).
**Les Saintes-Maries-de-la-Mer,
Camargue** Romany gypsies honour
effigies paraded from the ancient
church to the sea (late May).
Camargue *Ferrade*, spring round-
up and branding of one-year-old
Camargue bulls; the *gardians*

'cowboys' hold
horse-races.
St-Émilion The
Jurade *confrérie* has
a Spring festival (mid-June) and
proclaims the *Bans des Vendanges*
(grape harvest) (mid-September)
Juan-les-Pins, Côte d'Azur Jazz
festival (late July).
Aix-en-Provence Music and opera
festival (late July).
Avignon International theatre
festival (late July).
Frontignan, Languedoc *Festival du
Muscat* (wine) (July).
Languedoc villages including
Pézenas, Besson, Lodève, St-Jean-
de-Fos (and the town of Béziers):
totem parades, ancient village
games, traditional pantomimes (*fêtes
patronales*) (Ascension Day, 15 August
– check dates at
local tourist
offices).
Carcassonne
Spectacular
medieval
festival (early
August).
**Languedoc
coast** Sète,
Agde, Sérignan
Plage etc, boat-
jousting (all
summer).
**St-Chinian,
Languedoc** *Fête du Vin Nouveau* (wine)
(early November).
Major Alpine resorts Ski championships (December–March).

Alsace and Lorraine

Strasbourg Traditional Christmas
market (December).
Summer wine festivals Tokay,
Obermohschwihr (early July), Pinot
Noir, Rodem (late July),
Gewürztraminer, Bergheim (early
August).

Monte-Carlo rally

Carcassonne

Bare necessities

Greetings

good morning/good afternoon (to a man/woman/young girl)	**bonjour (Monsieur/Madame/ Mademoiselle)**
good evening/good night	**bonsoir/bonne nuit**
Bye!/Hi (informal)	**Salut!**
How are you?	**Comment allez-vous?**
How are things?	**Comment ça va?**
Fine, and you?	**Ça va! Et vous?**
See you later!	**À tout à l'heure!**
See you tomorrow!	**À demain!**
goodbye	**au revoir**

Other useful words

excuse me	**excusez-moi/pardon**
please	**s'il vous plaît**
Thank you (very much).	**Merci (beaucoup).**
You're very kind.	**Vous êtes très aimable.**
You're welcome.	**De rien.**
I'm sorry.	**Je suis désolé/e.**
yes/no	**oui/non**
OK	**OK!/D'accord.**
No, thank you.	**Non, merci.**

Is/are there . . . ?

Is there a lift?	**Il y a un ascenseur?**
Are there any toilets?	**Il y a des toilettes?**

Where is/are . . . ?

Where is the town centre?	**Où est le centre-ville?**
Where are the shoes?	**Où sont les chaussures?**

C'est (à droite/à gauche).   It's (on the right/on the left).

Do you have any . . . ?

Do you have any (sandwiches/cheese)?	**Avez-vous (des sandwichs/ du fromage)?**

How much . . . ?

How much/How many?	**Combien?**
How much is that?	**Ça fait combien?**

I'd like . . .

I'd like (a T-shirt/a melon).	**Je voudrais (un T-shirt/un melon).**
I'd like a kilo of (apples/carrots).	**Je voudrais un kilo de (pommes/ carottes).**

Autre chose?   Anything else?

Getting things straight

Pardon?	**Comment?**
Could you say that again?	**Pourriez-vous répéter?**
Could you speak (more) slowly, please?	**Parlez (plus) lentement, s'il vous plaît.**
I don't understand.	**Je ne comprends pas.**
I understand.	**Je comprends.**
Could you write it down?	**Pourriez-vous l'écrire?**
Do you speak (English)?	**Vous parlez (anglais)?**

About yourself

My name is . . .	**Je m'appelle . . .**
I'm Irish.	**Je suis irlandais/e.**
I'm from Glasgow.	**Je suis de Glasgow.**
(See p35 for a list of nationalities.)	
I'm a student.	**Je suis étudiant/e.**
I'm (married/divorced/ a widow/er).	**Je suis (marié/e/divorcé/e/ veuve/veuf).**
I speak a little French.	**Je parle un peu français.**

About other people

What's your name?	**Comment vous appelez-vous?**
May I introduce (Jill/my wife/ my husband)?	**Je vous présente (Jill/ma femme/ mon mari).**
Pleased to meet you.	**Enchanté!**
Where are you from?	**D'où êtes-vous?**
Would you like (a drink/to take a stroll)?	**Voulez-vous (prendre un verre/ faire une balade)?**
Are you on holiday?	**Vous êtes en vacances?**

Money

a . . . note	**un billet de . . .**
20 francs	**vingt francs**
500 francs	**cinq cents francs**
a . . . coin	**une pièce de . . .**
ten centimes	**dix centimes**
one franc	**un franc**
two francs	**deux francs**
Can you change a 100-franc note?	**Pouvez-vous me faire la monnaie de cent francs?**

(See p34 for Numbers.)

Changing money

I'd like to change (50) pounds into francs.	**Je voudrais changer (cinquante) livres en francs.**
exchange rate	**le taux de change**
commission	**la commission**
traveller's cheques	**les travellers/ chèques de voyage**

The time

Ouvert tous
les jours sauf
le mardi de
10 h à 18 h.

What time is it?	**Quelle heure est-il?**
What time does (the train leave/ the shop open)?	**À quelle heure (part le train/ ouvre le magasin)?**

Il est quatorze heures trente.	It's 14.30.
Il est zéro heure quinze.	It's quarter past midnight.
Dans cinq minutes.	In five minutes.
Dans trois heures.	In three hours.
Il est une heure (et quart/ et demie).	It's (quarter past/half past) one.
Pas avant cinq heures (moins vingt).	Not until (twenty to) five.
Jusqu'à dix heures (vingt-cinq).	Until (twenty-five past) ten.
À (midi/minuit).	At (noon/midnight).
À partir de six heures.	From six o'clock.

Alphabet

In French the letters of the alphabet are pronounced as follows.

A (ah)	**H** (ash)	**O** (oh)	**V** (vay)
B (bay)	**I** (ee)	**P** (pay)	**W** (doobluh vay)
C (say)	**J** (jee)	**Q** (kew)	**X** (eex)
D (day)	**K** (kah)	**R** (air)	**Y** (ee grek)
E (uh)	**L** (ell)	**S** (ess)	**Z** (zed)
F (eff)	**M** (em)	**T** (tay)	
G (jay)	**N** (en)	**U** (ew)	

Numbers

0	zéro	21	vingt et un
1	un	22	vingt-deux
2	deux	30	trente
3	trois	31	trente et un
4	quatre	40	quarante
5	cinq	50	cinquante
6	six	60	soixante
7	sept	70	soixante-dix
8	huit	71	soixante et
9	neuf		onze
10	dix	72	soixante-douze
11	onze	80	quatre-vingts
12	douze	81	quatre-vingt-un
13	treize	90	quatre-vingt-dix
14	quatorze	91	quatre-vingt-
15	quinze		onze
16	seize	100	cent
17	dix-sept	101	cent un
18	dix-huit	102	cent deux
19	dix-neuf	200	deux cents
20	vingt	2,000	deux mille

Ordinal numbers

1st	premier/première
2nd	deuxième
3rd	troisième
4th	quatrième
5th	cinquième

Colours

blue	bleu/e
black	noir/e
brown	marron
green	vert/e
grey	gris/e
orange	orange
pink	rose
red	rouge
white	blanc/he
yellow	jaune
plain	uni/e
patterned	à motifs
light	clair/e
dark	foncé/e

Countries and nationalities

Australia	**l'Australie: Australien/ne**
Austria	**l'Autriche: Autrichien/ne**
Belgium	**la Belgique: Belge**
Canada	**le Canada: Canadien/ne**
China	**la Chine: Chinois/e**
Denmark	**le Danemark: Danois/e**
England	**l'Angleterre: Anglais/e**
Finland	**la Finlande: Finlandais/e/Finnois/e**
France	**la France: Français/e**
Germany	**l'Allemagne: Allemand/e**
Greece	**la Grèce: Grec/que**
India	**l'Inde: Indien/ne**
Ireland	**l'Irlande: Irlandais/e**
Italy	**l'Italie: Italien/ne**
Japan	**le Japon: Japonais/e**
Luxembourg	**le Luxembourg: Luxembourgeois/e**
Netherlands/	**les Pays-Bas: Néerlandais/e /**
Holland	**la Hollande: Hollandais/e**
New Zealand	**la Nouvelle-Zélande: Néo-Zélandais/e**
Northern Ireland	**l'Irlande du Nord: Irlandais/e**
Norway	**la Norvège: Norvégien/ne**
Portugal	**le Portugal: Portugais/e**
Russia	**la Russie: Russe**
Scotland	**l'Écosse: Écossais/e**
South Africa	**l'Afrique du Sud: Sud-Africain/e**
Spain	**l'Espagne: Espagnol/e**
Sweden	**la Suède: Suédois/e**
Switzerland	**la Suisse: Suisse**
United States	**les États-Unis: Américain/e**
Wales	**le Pays de Galles: Gallois/e**

Days

Monday	**lundi**		today	**aujourd'hui**
Tuesday	**mardi**		tomorrow	**demain**
Wednesday	**mercredi**		yesterday	**hier**
Thursday	**jeudi**		morning	**le matin**
Friday	**vendredi**		afternoon	**l'après-midi**
Saturday	**samedi**		evening	**le soir**
Sunday	**dimanche**		week	**une semaine**

Months

January	**janvier**		July	**juillet**
February	**février**		August	**août**
March	**mars**		September	**septembre**
April	**avril**		October	**octobre**
May	**mai**		November	**novembre**
June	**juin**		December	**décembre**

Language works

Changing money

1 At the bank
- Bonjour.
- Bonjour Mademoiselle. Je voudrais changer quarante livres en francs s'il vous plaît.
- Oui, le taux de change est à huit francs trente-neuf. La commission est trente francs.
- D'accord.
- Voilà, trois cent cinq francs et six centimes.

The exchange rate's . . .
£40 is worth . . .

Getting things straight

2 At the market: understanding prices
- Voilà! Les pommes et les carottes. Autre chose?
- Non, merci. Ça fait combien?
- Alors, ça fait vingt-quatre soixante-cinq.
- Je suis désolé, je ne comprends pas. Pourriez-vous l'écrire?
- D'accord. Voilà!

The apples and carrots cost . . .

Try it out

As if you were there

Getting to know someone, in Provence. Fill in the replies.
- Bonjour, comment allez-vous?
- (Say good afternoon, you're well, and ask after him)
- Ça va, merci. Vous êtes en vacances?
- (Say yes, you're from . . . and your name's . . . Introduce your companion)
- Enchanté! Je m'appelle Paul. Voulez-vous prendre un verre?
- (Say yes, thank you very much!)

Crossed lines

Match the questions with the correct answers
1 Comment ça va?
2 D'où êtes-vous?
3 Vous parlez anglais?
4 À quelle heure part le train?

a Je parle un peu l'anglais.
b Ça va, et vous?
c Dans deux heures.
d Je suis de Paris.

Sound Check

c is pronounced in two ways, depending on the letter which follows it:
ç, c + e, i or **h** – like 's' in 'soft'

ça va	sah vah
cent	soh

c otherwise – like 'c' in 'can'

comment	commaw
d'accord	dacawr

Practise on these words:
commission, vacances, changer

Getting around

France is large and empty by European standards – save time by taking the motorway, high-speed trains or domestic flights for long hops, and explore the back roads at leisure, by car or bike. Inter-regional links are improving but a detour via Paris is sometimes simpler. Invest in Michelin's yellow maps of the region (as opposed to individual departments or smaller areas) you'll be visiting.

Arriving in France

Drivers can join the motorway from all international airports, plus the Channel ports of Calais, Boulogne and Le Havre. Roscoff and St-Malo (Brittany) and Cherbourg and Dieppe (Normandy) are on *routes nationales* (see below). Paris Charles-de-Gaulle / Roissy and Orly airports have direct rail and coach links to the centre of Paris.

Driving in France

Drivers are well catered for but accident statistics are alarming – be warned! Unmarked T-junctions on town and country roads have *priorité à droite* (give way to the right and hope everyone else does, too). Roundabout etiquette is seldom observed, and people rarely indicate. Don't worry if drivers flash their lights – this is the standard warning of a speed radar or police road check ahead! Night radars take a flash photograph of your number plate. Road signs mostly follow standard international styles. Watch out for STOP signs, as distinct from *Cédez le passage* (Give Way). Also *verglas* (black ice), *ralentir* (reduce speed), *sauf riverains* (residents and deliveries only). Don't forget you can put your car on the train for a long hop (ask your travel agent, or at the station information office). **International car hire companies** have desks in all airports, most towns and major train stations. Check for distance restrictions – ask for unlimited kilometres (*kilométrage illimité*) if in doubt. Pay any fines to your hirer – they will deal with the paperwork.

❙ I'd like to hire a car, please.
● **Je voudrais louer une voiture, s'il vous plaît.**

Petrol

Diesel (*gasoil* or *gazole*) in particular is quite cheap. Supermarket service stations often have automatic 24-hour pumps (Visa or Mastercard); smaller garages tend to close on Sundays and early evenings; remote regions can be quite 'dry' – watch your fuel gauge.

Traffic information

French regions stagger school breaks to relieve traffic pressure, but motorways out of major cities are always blocked on the main national holidays. Precise dates vary; black spots are late October to early November, Christmas and New Year, February, Easter week, Pentecost (late May), early and mid-July and 15–30 August. Local and national traffic news is on 107.7FM, with English bulletins in summer.

Les autoroutes

The *autoroutes* (motorways) are mostly numbered clockwise around Paris starting with the A1, which runs north. They are free around major cities, after which tolls (*le péage*) operate. Collect a ticket and pay at the next toll. Larger *péages* have manned and automated lanes (Visa and Mastercard), cash-only and subscribers' lanes. Motorway driving is fast, often with only two lanes in each direction – take care. Frequent rest areas (*les aires de repos*) range from basic toilets and drinking-water (*eau potable*) to service stations with motels, mini-supermarkets, restaurants, picnic tables, play areas, even public fax machines. Look out for the brown signs indicating local sights and curiosities.

Les nationales

The national N-roads, also numbered clockwise from Paris, are fine for touring but frustrating if you're in a hurry – they are often small and jammed through town centres (ring roads are a rarity).

Les départementales

Often quiet and attractive roads, D-road numbers change between departments. All numbers are marked on the top of signposts and on yellow-and-white roadside kilometre markers (*bornes*).

Chemins communaux

C-roads are small country and village lanes.

Taking the train

All railway stations are signposted Gare SNCF. France's famous high-speed train, the TGV (up to 186 miles per hour), connects Paris with

European and regional cities. Features include *couchettes*, telephones and special seats and toilets for wheelchair users.

Information and reservations offices (at the 'i' sign) in all main stations cover the TGV and other main-line routes (*grandes lignes*), with free timetables including information in English, local maps and station guides. Local tickets can be bought from machines (*Billeterie automatique*), or the ticket office (*au guichet*). Stamp your ticket (*composter le billet*) at the platform machines – otherwise it's invalid.

PRIERE DE NE PAS STATIONNER · SORTIE DE VOITURES

Special fares (*tarifs spéciaux*) exist for young people, students, seniors, couples, families, off-peak hours (*période bleue*).

🚶 Have you got a timetable?
Avez-vous un horaire?

Coaches and buses

Connections between neighbouring towns and cities can prove more convenient than trains – ask for *correspondances autocar* (coach connections) at information offices.

Local bus services run from the central bus station (*gare routière*) in all main towns. Town centres and suburbs are usually well served, rural areas less so (sometimes not at all or

only at school times, around 7.30 am and 5 pm). Tickets can be bought at a tobacconist's (*un tabac*). A book of tickets (*un carnet*) may be cheaper for frequent local trips. Remember to stamp your ticket if there is a machine on board.

Sponsored free coach services sometimes operate between regional capitals during the summer. Ask at local tourist offices.

🚶 Are there any buses to Lyon, please?
Il y a des bus pour Lyon, s'il vous plaît?

Internal flights

Major regional airports have frequent shuttle services to Paris (mostly Orly). Air Inter, the state domestic airline, no longer has a monopoly – shop around (try TAT and AOM). You can buy tickets on the spot. Prices are competitive, with the usual discounts for young people, off-peak travel etc.

Boating

Popular options include the Canal du Midi (from Toulouse to the Mediterranean at Agde), the canal system linking St-Malo, Nantes and Rennes in Brittany, and gentle rivers such as the Seine and the Loire.

Travelling with children

Parent-and-baby rooms or changing tables in ladies' toilets are found at most motorway services, on domestic flights and on the TGV. *Relais Bébé* (baby stops) on motorways from June to early September are sponsored by Nestlé, offering free nappies, baby food and mineral water.

Motorway play areas are clearly signposted – often you'll find some of the best playgrounds in France! Some rest areas offer children's entertainment in the summer. Details are broadcast on 107.7FM.

🚶 Where is the nearest baby stop, please?
Où est le relais bébé le plus proche, s'il vous plaît?

CIRCULATION INTERDITE

SAUF BUS

TOUTES DIRECTIONS

Phrasemaker
Asking the way

Excuse me, (sir/madam).	**Pardon, (Monsieur/Madame).**
Which way is (the station/ the town centre)?	**Pour aller (à la gare/au centre-ville), s'il vous plaît?**
Is it (very) far?	**C'est (très) loin?**
Is there (a bank/a park) near here?	**Il y a (une banque/un jardin public) près d'ici?**
Is this the right way (to the town centre/to the station)?	**C'est le chemin (du centre-ville/de la gare)?**

C'est là!	There it is!
tournez (à droite/à gauche)	turn (right/left)
c'est (à droite/à gauche)	it's (on the right/on the left)
traversez la rue	cross the street
(allez/continuez) tout droit	(go/carry) straight on
passez le pont	cross the bridge
prenez la première rue à droite	take the first street on the right
jusqu'au rond point	as far as the roundabout
C'est à (environ) cent mètres.	It's (about) 100 metres away.
au bout de la rue	at the end of the street
C'est au coin.	It's on the corner.
C'est (assez) près/en face/ derrière.	It's (quite) near/ opposite/ behind.
passage (pour piétons/clouté)	pedestrian crossing

Places to look for

See p58 for a list of French shops.

airport	**l'aéroport**	(pedestrian) street	**la rue (piétonne)**
bank	**la banque**	petrol station	**station d'essence**
beach	**la plage**	police station	**le commissariat de police**
boulevard	**le boulevard**		
bridge	**le pont**		
bus station	**la gare d'auto-bus**	post office	**la poste**
		public toilets	**les toilettes publiques**
bus stop	**l'arrêt d'auto-bus (m)**		
		shopping centre	**le centre commercial**
castle	**le château**		
cathedral	**la cathédrale**	square	**la place**
chemist's	**la pharmacie**	stadium	**le stade**
church	**l'église (f)**	station	**la gare**
city walls	**les remparts**	swimming pool	**la piscine**
coach station	**la gare routière**	taxi rank	**la station de taxis**
hospital	**l'hôpital (m)**		
museum	**le musée**	tower	**la tour**
park	**le jardin public**	traffic lights	**les feux rouges**
port	**le port**		

Road signs

autoroute (à péage)	(toll) motorway
Attention!	Watch out!
cédez le passage	give way
centre-ville	town centre
gravillons	loose chippings
passage protégé	right of way
poids lourds	heavy-goods vehicles
priorité à droite	give way to the right
ralentir	slow down
rappel	speed limit reminder
serrez à droite	keep to the right
sortie	exit
stationnement interdit	no parking

Hiring a car or bike

Car hire	**Location de (voitures/autos)**
I'd like to hire . . .	**Je voudrais louer . . .**
a (small/large) car	**une (petite/grande) voiture**
a bike	**un vélo**
for (two days/a week)	**pour (deux jours/une semaine)**
How much is it (per day/ per week)?	**C'est combien (par jour/ par semaine)?**
Is it unlimited mileage?	**C'est kilométrage illimité?**
Is insurance included?	**L'assurance est comprise?**

Pour combien de jours?	For how many days?
Qui va conduire?	Who'll be driving?
Votre permis, s'il vous plaît.	Your driving licence, please.

Buying petrol

30 litres of (unleaded/diesel/4-star).	**Trente litres de (sans plomb/gasoil/super).**
Fill up with . . .	**Faites le plein de . . .**
Have you got any (air/water/oil)?	**Vous avez de (l'air/l'eau/l'huile)?**
How much is it?	**Ça fait combien?**
Is it self-service?	**C'est self-service?**

Roadside information

Is this the right way to Dijon?	**C'est bien la route de Dijon?**
How many kilometres to Dijon?	**Dijon est à combien de kilomètres?**

Using the underground

one ticket	**un ticket**
book of tickets	**un carnet**
special tourist ticket	**un billet touriste**
Does this train go to Paris?	**Ce train va à Paris?**
Which line do I need for Bastille?	**Quelle ligne pour Bastille?**

Il faut changer à l'Étoile.	You need to change at l'Étoile.
Prenez la ligne rouge.	Take the red line.

boat	**le bateau**	crossing	**la traversée**
bus	**le bus**	ferry	**le ferry**
cable car	**le téléphérique**	flight	**le vol**
car	**la voiture**	hydrofoil	**l'hydrofoil**
coach	**le car**	plane	**l'avion**
connection	**la correspon-dance**	shuttle service	**la navette**
		train	**le train**

Catching a taxi

To (this address/the airport).	**À (cette adresse/l'aéroport).**
Quickly, please!	**Vite, s'il vous plaît!**
How long will it take?	**Combien de temps ça prendra?**
I'd like a receipt.	**Je voudrais un reçu.**

Ce n'est pas loin/C'est assez loin.	It's not far/quite a way.
Pas longtemps.	Not long.

Getting information on trains and buses

Are there any (buses/trains) to . . . ?	**Il y a des (bus/trains) pour . . . ?**
What time does the bus (leave/arrive)?	**Le bus (part/arrive) à quelle heure?**
What time does the (last/next) train leave?	**(Le dernier/Le prochain) train part à quelle heure?**
Which platform?	**Quel quai?**
How long does it take?	**Ça prend combien de temps?**
Have you got a timetable?	**Avez-vous un horaire?**
Does it stop at . . . ?	**Il s'arrête à . . . ?**
Where must I get off?	**A quel arrêt dois-je descendre?**

Descendez à . . .	Get off at . . .
Il faut changer à . . .	You must change at . . .
Il y a une correspondance.	There's a connection.
Je vais vous montrer.	I'll show you.

Buying a ticket

Where's the ticket office?	**Où est le guichet,?**
a (return/single) ticket to Paris	**un (aller-retour/aller simple) pour Paris**
for two adults and one child	**pour deux adultes et un enfant**
first/second class	**première/deuxième classe**
I'd like to reserve (a seat/a couchette).	**Je voudrais réserver (une place/une couchette).**

Fumeur ou non-fumeur?	Smoking or non-smoking?
Il y a un supplément de . . . francs.	There's a . . . -franc supplement.
N'oubliez pas de composter.	Don't forget to validate your ticket.

Sound Check

Take care to distinguish between the sounds **oi** and **oy** and **ui**

voiture	vwatewr
patinoire	pateenwar
droite	drwat

but

hydrofoil	hydrofoil
voyage	vwhyaj
huile	weel
conduire	condweer

Practise on these words: **trois, voie, fruit**

Language works

Asking your way

1 Asking the way to the nearest chemist's
- **Pardon, Madame, il y a une pharmacie près d'ici, s'il vous plaît?**
- □ **Oui. Allez tout droit, jusqu'aux feux, traversez la rue, continuez et prenez la première rue à droite. La pharmacie est dans la rue piétonne.**
- **Merci beaucoup.**

The chemist's is before/after the traffic lights.

Hiring a car

2 Hiring a small car
- **Bonjour. Je voudrais louer une petite voiture. C'est combien par jour?**
- □ **C'est quatre cents francs par jour.**
- **Kilométrage illimité?**
- □ **Oui. Votre permis, s'il vous plaît.**

What did the assistant ask to see?

Getting petrol and roadside information

3 Filling up with petrol and asking the way to the motorway
- **Bonjour. Ce n'est pas self-service.**
- □ **Pardon, faites le plein de sans plomb, s'il vous plaît.**
- **Voilà. Autre chose?**
- □ **Non, merci. L'autoroute est à combien de kilomètres?**
- **Environ quinze kilomètres. Attention! Il y a un péage!**

The driver was warned about road works/bridge/toll.

Getting information on trains

4 Travelling to Saint Tropez
- **Le prochain train pour St-Tropez part à quelle heure?**
- □ **Quatorze heures vingt-huit. Il faut changer à Nice.**
- **Ça prend combien de temps?**
- □ **Trois heures.**

The train leaves at . . . and is/isn't direct.

Buying a ticket

5 Buying return tickets for the family

- **Bonjour, trois allers-retours pour Blois: deux adultes et un enfant.**
- **Première ou deuxième classe?**
- **Oh! Deuxième classe!**
- **Bon, voilà. Trois billets: deux adultes, un enfant.**
- **Quel quai, s'il vous plaît?**
- **Quai huit . . . N'oubliez pas de composter!**

Platform number . . .
Don't forget to . . .

⊘ Orientation	
→	
Départ grandes lignes	Main line departure
Billets	Tickets
ⓘ Information	
ⓖ Réservation	
ⓔ Objets trouvés	
ⓢ Service après vente	After-sale service
ⓡ Retrait des bagages	Luggage retrieval
ⓒ Consigne manuelle	Left luggage office
ⓣ Toilettes	
ⓔ Change	
ⓛ Location de voitures	Car rental
ⓞ Office de tourisme	Tourist information

Try it out

What's missing?

Fill in the missing letters to make four French phrases
1 Straight on: **t_ _ _ d_ _ _ _.**
2 Cross the bridge: **passez le p_ _ _.**
3 Fill her up, please: **f_ _ _ _ _ le p_ _ _, s'il vous plaît.**
4 I'd like to hire a car: **je voudrais _ _ _ _ _ une v_ _ _ _ _ _.**

As if you were there

Asking the way in a car
- (Say excuse me and ask if there's a petrol station nearby)
- **Oui, c'est près du centre commercial. Continuez jusqu'au rond-point. C'est au coin, à gauche.**
- (Say thanks and ask for directions to the southbound motorway)
- **À cent mètres du centre commercial, passez le pont. Allez tout droit. L'autoroute se trouve là-bas.**
- (Ask if there's a toll)
- **Ah oui! Malheureusement!**

Somewhere to stay

Information and booking

French tourist offices abroad provide information on all accommodation types, sometimes with booking services (also main regional offices in France).

Book ahead in French school holidays: February–early March (avoid ski resorts), Easter, May bank holiday weekends, early July to late August, end October–early November, and Christmas. No need to book hotels out of season (but pot luck may not ensure charm – ask to see rooms first). *Chambres d'hôtes* (B&Bs) and farmhouse rooms may not be available at short notice – call in if you're passing, otherwise telephone first. *Gîtes* (self-catering cottages) must be booked ahead.

🕴 Can I see the room, please?
🔴 **Je peux voir la chambre, s'il**
🔴 **vous plaît?**

Hotels

France offers everything from plain establishments on village squares, to châteaux, alpine chalets or modern chains (Ibis, Mercure, Pullman, Campanile etc). Most offer good

value for money. Many have family rooms with double and single beds, and provide extra beds or cots (supplementary charge). Room prices and facilities must be listed on the back of each room's door and NN (*nouvelles normes*) Star ratings (where given) range from zero to four. Look out for members of *Relais et Châteaux, Demeures et Châteaux, Logis de France* (over 4,000 family-run hotel-restaurants – 'chimney-piece' symbol and rating system) and *Relais du Silence* (quiet country hotels). Motorway hotels are useful stopovers on a long haul. Rooms usually sleep up to three (one double, one single bed). Chains include *Formule 1, Fast'hôtel* and *Bonsaï*.

Self-catering and farm stay holidays

Gîtes de France ('ear of corn' rating) offer farm camping (*camping à la ferme*), self-catering and bed-and-breakfast (sometimes dinner) (*chambres d'hôtes*). Contact your nearest French tourist office for brochures and lists of other holiday lets (*locations saisonnières*). Specify which regions you are interested in. Look out for *Gîtes de Pêche* (anglers), *Gîtes de Neige* (ski resorts), *Gîtes et Chevaux* (horse-back treks), *Gîtes Panda* (wildlife watching in national parks). Sheets are not provided unless requested. *Gîtes d'étape* and mountain *refuges* (huts) provide dormitory or family rooms and home cooking in remote areas, often on long-distance footpaths. Use *Bienvenue à la ferme* ('sunflower' rating) for farm stay holidays featuring farm tours, teas (*les goûters à la ferme*), game shooting (*la chasse*) and produce sold direct from the farm. Tourist offices carry brochures detailing local members. Check out *les fermes-auberges* (farmhouse restaurants offering home-cooked regional specialities and farm produce), *les fermes équestres* (for riding and trekking holidays including beginners), *les fermes de séjour* (for bed, breakfast and home-cooked dinner – maximum six guest rooms) and *les campings en ferme d'accueil* (small, quiet, well-equipped farm campsites offering group suppers and outings).

St-Paul-de-Vence, Côte d'Azur

Can I hire some sheets?
Je peux louer des draps?

Camping and villages de vacances

Basic *campings municipaux* (municipal campsites) exist throughout France. Summer resorts have privately-run, star-rated campsites with pools, sports facilities, shops, restaurants, nightclubs etc. Many have electric points for motor-homes (*les camping-cars*), and rent bungalows or mobile homes.

    Aires naturelles de camping are the simplest of all sites. *Villages de vacances*, with individual chalets, barbecues etc. are a popular alternative to camping. Chains include *Campotel/ Logivert* and *Villages Vacances Familiales*.

Do you have a pitch for one tent available?
Vous avez un emplacement de libre pour une tente?

Useful addresses

Maison des Gîtes de France
59 rue St-Lazare, 75439 Paris Cedex 09
(01) 49 70 75 75
178 Piccadilly, London, W1
(0171) 493 3480
Relais et Châteaux
15 rue Galvani, 75017 Paris
(01) 45 72 90 00
A.P.C.A. (*Bienvenue à la Ferme* handbook)
9 av Georges-V, 75008 Paris
(01) 47 23 55 40

Phrasemaker

Finding a place

Is there (a hotel/a campsite) near here?	Il y a (un hôtel/un camping) près d'ici?
Do you have a room available?	Vous avez une chambre de libre?
I'd like a room for (tonight/three nights).	Je voudrais une chambre pour (ce soir/trois nuits).
a (single/double/family) room	une chambre (pour une personne/à grand lit/de famille)
for four people – two adults and two children	pour quatre personnes – deux adultes et deux enfants
Can I see the room?	Je peux voir la chambre?
How much is it per night?	C'est combien par nuit?
Do you have anything cheaper?	Vous en avez une moins cher?
I'll think about it.	Je vais réfléchir.
OK, I'll take it.	OK, je la prends.

Pour combien de nuits?	For how many nights?
Que voulez-vous comme chambre?	What sort of room do you want?
Pour combien de personnes?	For how many people?
Désolé, c'est complet.	Sorry, we're full.
Demi-tarif pour les enfants.	Children are half price.

Places to stay

bed and breakfast	une chambre d'hôte
campsite	un terrain de camping
farmhouse	une ferme
guest house/boarding house	une pension
hotel	un hôtel
rented room	une chambre louée
self-catering (flat/cottage)	(un appartement/un chalet) loué
youth hostel	une auberge de jeunesse

Specifications

with a (shower/bath)	**avec (douche/bain)**
with a (bathroom/cot)	**avec (salle de bains/lit d'enfant)**
Could you add an extra bed?	**Pourriez-vous ajouter un autre lit?**
Is breakfast included?	**Le petit déjeuner est compris?**

Le petit déjeuner est (en supplément/compris). Breakfast is (extra/included).

Toutes taxes comprises/TTC. All taxes are included.

La Roque Gageac, Dordogne

Checking in

I have a reservation.	**J'ai une réservation.**
My name's Smith.	**Mon nom est Smith.**
Where can (I/we) park?	**Où peut-on se garer?**

Votre (nom/passeport), s'il vous plaît. Your (name/passport), please.

Pourriez-vous remplir la fiche? Please fill in this form.

Pourriez-vous l'écrire? Could you write it down?

Quel est votre numéro d'immatriculation? What's your car's registration number?

Chambre vingt-quatre, au deuxième étage. Room 24, on the second floor.

Checking out

I'd like to pay the bill.	**Je voudrais payer ma note.**
with traveller's cheques/ by credit card/with cash.	**avec travellers/avec une carte de crédit/en espèces.**
There's a mistake.	**Il y a une erreur.**

Services

What time is breakfast?	**À quelle heure est le petit déjeuner?**
I'd like breakfast in my room.	**Je voudrais le petit déjeuner dans ma chambre.**
Do you have an iron?	**Avez-vous un fer à repasser?**
Where is (the restaurant/the bar)?	**Où est (le restaurant/le bar)?**
Is there (a lift/air-conditioning)?	**Il y a (un ascenseur/la climatisation)?**
Le petit déjeuner est de sept heures à huit heures et demie. au (rez-de-chaussée/premier/deuxième étage)	Breakfast is from 7.00am to 8.30am. on the (ground floor/first/second floor)

Signs

demi-pension	half board
ne pas déranger	do not disturb
fermé	closed
interdit/défense d'entrer	no entry
occupé	engaged
ouvert	open
en panne	out of order
stationnement réservé aux (riverains/clients)	(residents'/customers') parking only
table d'hôte	evening meal provided

Asking for help

Could I have an alarm call at . . .?	**Pourriez-vous me réveiller à . . . ?**
Have you got a safe deposit box?	**Avez-vous un coffre-fort?**
Do you have a plan of the town?	**Avez-vous un plan de la ville?**
Could you recommend a restaurant?	**Connaissez-vous un bon restaurant?**
Could you order me a taxi?	**Pourriez-vous m'appeler un taxi?**
Could I have (a key/another towel) please?	**Pourrais-je avoir (une clé/une autre serviette)?**
How do I get an outside number?	**Comment obtenir une ligne extérieure?**
Dial (zero).	**Faites le (zéro).**

At the campsite

Do you have a pitch available . . .

for (a caravan/a caravanette/ a tent)?
How much is it per night?
Here's my camping carnet.

Vous avez un emplacement de libre . . .

pour (une caravane/un camping-car/une tente)?
C'est combien par nuit?
Voilà mon carnet.

La redevance campeur est de vingt-cinq francs.
The camper's fee is 25 francs.

Une taxe de séjour de six francs (par nuitée/par personne).
Tourists' tax is six francs (per night/per person).

Canal du Midi

Signs

camp gardé — secure campsite
douche (froide/chaude) — (cold/hot) shower
eau (potable/non potable) — (drinking/not drinking) water
interdit de camper ici — camping forbidden in this area
réservé aux caravanes — caravans only

Self-catering and youth hostels

I'd like to rent (the flat/ the house).
When are the dustbins emptied?

Are there any additional costs?
Can I hire (a sleeping bag/ some sheets)?
What time do you lock up?

Je voudrais louer (l'appartement/ la maison).
Quel jour ramasse-t-on les ordures?
Il y a des charges en supplément?
Je peux louer (un sac de couchage/des draps)?
À quelle heure vous fermez?

Il y a un compteur.
There's a meter.

Toutes taxes comprises/TTC.
All taxes included.

Problems

There's a problem with (the shower/the lamp).	**Il y a un problème avec (la douche/la lampe).**
The room's very cold.	**La chambre est glacée.**
There's no (soap/toilet paper/(hot) water).	**Il n'y a pas (de savon/de papier de toilette/d'eau (chaude)).**

Je vais envoyer quelqu'un.	I'll send somebody.
On vous en apporte.	We'll get you some.

bath	**la baignoire**	lighting	**la lumière**
bed	**le lit**	lock	**la serrure**
bidet	**le bidet**	plug	**le bouchon**
blankets	**les couvertures**	shower	**la douche**
blinds	**les stores**	shutters	**les volets**
boiler	**la chaudière**	tap	**le robinet**
central heating	**le chauffage central**	(bath) towel	**la serviette (de bain)**
cooker	**la cuisinière**	telephone	**le téléphone**
curtain	**le rideau**	ventilation	**l'aération**
drainage	**l'égout**	wash basin	**le lavabo**
electricity	**l'électricité**	window	**la fenêtre**
hangers	**les cintres**		

Sound Check

Take care to distinguish between the sounds **ai**, **aî** and **ail**

plaît	pleh
fraîche	fresh
j'ai	jay
baignoire	baynywar
travail	travaye

Practise on these words: **saison**, **voudrais**

Language works

Finding a place

1 Looking for a double room
- Bonjour Madame, vous avez une chambre de libre?
- Oui, une chambre à grand lit et une chambre pour une personne.
- Je peux voir la chambre à grand lit? (in the room) C'est combien?
- Deux cent francs.
- Le petit déjeuner est compris?
- Désolée, c'est en supplément.

The room costs . . .
Breakfast is/isn't included.

Checking in

2 Checking in to a reserved double room
- Bonjour, j'ai une réservation; mon nom est Marteau.
- Ah oui, Monsieur Marteau: une chambre à grand lit, avec salle de bains.
- Oui.
- Voilà, chambre douze, au premier étage.
- Merci. À quelle heure est le petit déjeuner?
- À partir de six heures et demie. Pourriez-vous remplir la fiche?

Breakfast is served from . . .

At the campsite

3 Finding out the cost of a pitch and the additional taxes
- Vous avez un emplacement pour une tente?
- Oui. Pour combien de nuits?
- Quatre nuits.
- Vous avez votre carnet?
- Voilà mon carnet. C'est combien?
- Emplacement: cinquante-cinq francs, redevance campeur: vingt-cinq francs, taxe de séjour: six francs par nuitée.

How much is it all together?

Self-catering

4 Finding out about renting a flat
- **Je voudrais louer l'appartement. C'est combien?**
- ☐ **C'est de quatre mille francs par semaine.**
- **L'électricité est comprise?**
- ☐ **Non, il y a un compteur.**
- **Je peux le voir?**
- ☐ **Oui, suivez-moi!**

(**Suivez-moi** = follow me)

The flat costs . . . francs a week.
Rent includes/doesn't include electricity.

Try it out

Mix and match

Match the phrases
to complete
the sentences
1 Désolé, c'est . . .
2 Pourriez-vous . . .
3 À quelle heure . . .
4 Une chambre . . .
5 Je peux . . .

a voir la chambre?
b à grand lit.
c complet.
d remplir la fiche?
e est le petit
déjeuner?

What's missing?

All the words start with C
1 No vacancies: _ _ _ _ _ _ _
2 Not cheap: _ _ _ _
3 How much? _ _ _ _ _ _ _
4 A room to sleep in: _ _ _ _ _ _ _

As if you were there

Looking for a room for two adults
- (Say good afternoon and you'd like a room)
- ☐ **Pour combien de personnes?**
- (Say for two adults)
- ☐ **Que voulez-vous comme chambre? Il y a une chambre à deux lits et il y a une chambre à grand lit.**
- (Say the room with the double bed, please)
- ☐ **Bon, d'accord. Pour combien de nuits?**
- (Say for three nights and ask how much it is per night and whether breakfast is included)
- ☐ **Deux cents cinquante. Le petit déjeuner est en supplément.**

Bergerac, Dordogne

Buying things

Shops

Local shops close on Mondays, and from around noon to 2 pm every day (even 4 pm in the south), but often stay open until 7.30 pm or 8 pm. Food shops often open on Sunday mornings. Many small shops close for public holidays, or during August (especially in the Paris region). Boxing Day and Good Friday are not holidays.

Most small shops will gift-wrap (*faire un paquet cadeau*) beautifully for free. Bargaining is not acceptable, even at the market.

Buying food

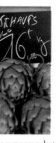

Use supermarkets for self-catering essentials and good value fresh fish, meat and poultry. Visit local markets for vegetables, fruit and specialities. Local bakeries, markets and delicatessens (*traiteurs*) are best for picnic fare: bread, pastries, dips, prepared salads, pâtés and *charcuterie*. Variations on the baguette include *une ficelle* (thinner), *un pain* (fatter), *un* (plaited or spiky version). Try *pain de campagne* (coarser flour), *complet* (wholemeal), *aux céréales* (granary), *aux noix* (with walnuts), *de seigle* (rye).

Une boule is a hefty, crusty, rich, round loaf and *fougasses* are delicious, flavoured breads made with bacon, olive oil and herbs, Roquefort or dried tomatoes.

! Do you have any granary bread?
● **Avez-vous du pain aux céréales?**

Best-value goods

Clothes and shoes (Even super-market labels) are stylish and competitive, with quality fabrics and leathers. French sizes tend to be small and children's clothes and shoes are irresistible but expensive. Hypermarkets stock delightful, cheap basics. Paris 'stock' shops sell cut-price couture (March and autumn), and ready-to-wear (July and January). Try rue St-Placide (6th arrondissement); also Stock Bourse (5-7 rue St-Augustin, 2nd arr.).

Luxury goods and French brands
Hermès, Les Must de Cartier, Villeroy et Boch, Le Creuset, perfumes etc can be cheaper in France (and duty free). Visit airport boutiques and *Printemps* or *Galeries Lafayette* stores throughout France.

Local specialities

Ceramics Look out for porcelain in Limoges, rustic and North African pottery in the south (pottery market at St-Jean-de-Fos in August) also wood-fired terracotta garden pots, floor and roof tiles. Faïence is made at Moustiers in Provence, and with distinctive naïve motifs, in Quimper, Brittany. Alsace has attractive cookware – look for kugelhopf moulds.

Glass Centres include Biot, north of Cannes – beautiful but pricey 'bubbled' glassware – and Couloubrines (Montpellier region). For crystal go to the Vosges, Arques (Calais region), La Rochère (Hautes-Alpes, France's oldest glassworks), and Passavant-la-Rochelle (Saône valley).

Natural soaps, perfumes, bath products Provence is the main centre; Marseille is famous for its soap (Le Chat) and there are several perfumiers in Grasse.

Carving You'll find olive-wood bowls, lamp bases etc in Provence; Basque craftsmen carve ornamental canes (*makila*); wooden toys are made in the Jura region (look for *JeuJura*) and woodcarving and furniture-making thrive in the pine-rich Alps and Queyras region.

Local delicacies

La Comtesse du Barry (in most towns or shopping centres) specialises in gift foods suitable for transporting home. Also Fauchon (26 place de la Madeleine, Paris, 8th arr.) and good *traiteurs* or supermarkets.

Tins or jars of *confits, cassoulet, choucroute, foie gras*, goose fat (great fo chips), goat's cheese in olive oil, pea smoked garlic, Provençal lavender honey, Bonne Maman jams, sauce

Also garlic strings, dried herbs, sea-salted butter from Brittany, Normandy cider and dried sausag

Sweets

Calais region *les bêtises de Cambrai* o *les Chuques du Nord*, coffee-caramel candies.

Languedoc *Berlingots de Pézenas*, hand-made, naturally-flavoured a coloured boiled sugar sweets.

Aix-en-Provence *calissons*, iced honey-and-almond sweetmeats.

Bordeaux region *canelés*, batter cak caramelised in tiny copper moulds

Provence *marrons glacés*, preserved sweet chestnuts.

Toulouse *violettes*, crystallised viole

Cheeses

You'll find most of these cheeses all over France, but do look out for local specialities:

Paris and the Loire Brie, made in Melun, Meaux, Nangis and Montereau, Crottin de Chavignol, Selles-sur-Cher (charcoal-dusted soft goat's cheese).

The Alps Morbier (the Jura), Gruyère, Emmenthal, Vacherin, Reblochon, Tomme de Savoie, St-Marcelin (hard cheeses).

The Massif Central Cantal, Salers, Saint-Nectaire, Fourme d'Ambert, Bleu d'Auvergne, Roquefort (blue, with ewe's milk).

Normandy Camembert, Pont-Évêque, Livarot.

The North Maroilles.

Wine

Self-caterers should 'fill up' with AOC or good-quality *vin du pays* (petrol-pump style) at the local *cave coopérative*, who also usually sell plastic containers (*bidons*) or bottles. Remember to decant from large containers (eg into empty mineral water bottles) once opened. Visitors to intensive wine regions (Bordeaux, Bourgogne) will need a good pocket guide with at-a-glance ratings on particular *châteaux* or *domaines*, best years etc, but here's a brief guide to labels.

Appellation d'Origine Contrôlée The AOC is a guarantee of quality and denotes wines from a clearly-defined area, made to certain specifications. The year of production is always indicated. Additional distinctions include *Grand Vin de Bordeaux*, *Grand Vin de Bourgogne* etc.

Vin du pays is non-AOC regional wine – often perfectly drinkable.

Vin de table is basic plonk.

Mis en bouteille au château (or *à la propriété*) – the wine is produced and bottled at a particular vineyard. Without this, labels refering to one property (or *domaine*) may indicate the grower of the grapes (the wine itself may be made or bottled elsewhere).

A private *négociant* or collective (*cave coopérative*) may buy in grapes from various growers – often perfectly good AOC, and cheaper.

How much is that?
Ça fait combien?

Livraison gratuite

Phrasemaker

Phrases to use anywhere

Do you have (any wholemeal bread/any stamps)?	**Avez-vous (du pain complet/ des timbres)?**
How much is that?	**Ça fait combien?**
I'd like . . . please.	**Je voudrais . . . s'il vous plaît.**
a bit (more/less)	**mettez (plus/moins)**
I'd like another.	**J'en voudrais (un/une) autre.**

May I try some?	**Je peux goûter?**
What is it?	**Qu'est-ce que c'est?**
(This/That) one.	**Ça.**
That's all.	**C'est tout.**
It's too expensive.	**C'est trop cher.**
Can I pay . . .	**Je peux payer . . .**
with a traveller's cheque?	**avec un (travellers/ cheque de voyage)?**
by credit card?	**avec une carte de crédit?**

Je peux vous aider?	Can I help you?
Désolé/e.	Sorry.
Voilà.	Here you are.
Combien en voulez-vous?	How (much/many) do you want?
Il n'en reste plus.	It's sold out.
Autre chose?	Anything else?
Ça fait . . . francs.	That's . . . francs, altogether.

Shops

butcher's	**une boucherie**	off-licence	**un débit de vins et spiritueux**
bakery	**une boulangerie**	delicatessen	**une charcuterie**
bookshop and stationer's	**une librairie-papeterie**	post office	**une poste**
cake shop	**une pâtisserie**	shopping centre	**un centre commercial**
chemist's	**une pharmacie**	tobacconist's	**un bureau de tabac**
department store	**un grand magasin**	travel agent's	**une agence de voyages**
(flea) market	**un marché (aux puces)**		
florist	**un fleuriste**		
general food store	**une alimentation générale**		
grocer's	**une épicerie**		
hairdressing salon	**un salon de coiffure**		
jeweller's	**une bijouterie**		
newsagent's	**un marchand de journaux**		

Quantities

a kilo	**un kilo**	a litre	**un litre**
half a kilo	**un demi-kilo**	half a litre	**un demi-litre**
100 grams	**cent grammes**	a third	**un tiers**
another	**un/une autre**	a quarter	**un quart**
bag of flour	**un sac de farine**	one piece of (cake)	**un morceau de (gâteau)**
bottle of wine	**une bouteille de vin**	packet of butter	**une plaquette de beurre**
can of lemonade	**une boîte de limonade**	packet of sweets	**un paquet de bonbons**
carton of milk	**un carton de lait**	slice of (ham)	**une tranche de (jambon)**
jar of jam	**un pot de confiture**	tube of toothpaste	**un tube de dentifrice**

Fruit

apple	**une pomme**	nectarine	**une nectarine**
apricot	**un abricot**	orange	**une orange**
banana	**une banane**	peach	**une pêche**
cherries	**les cerises**	pear	**une poire**
dates	**les dattes**	pineapple	**un ananas**
grapefruit	**un pamplemousse**	plum	**une prune**
		raspberries	**les framboises**
grapes	**le raisin**	strawberries	**les fraises**
lemon	**un citron**	water melon	**une pastèque**

Vegetables

artichoke	**un artichaut**	mushroom	**un champignon**
aubergine	**une aubergine**	olive	**une olive**
avocado	**un avocat**	onion	**un oignon**
cabbage	**un chou**	peas	**les petits pois**
carrot	**une carotte**	(red/green) pepper	**un poivron (rouge/vert)**
celery	**un céleri**	potatoes	**les pommes de terre**
chicory	**une endive**		
courgette	**une courgette**	radish	**un radis**
cucumber	**un concombre**	rocket salad	**la roquette**
French beans	**les haricots verts**	shallot	**une échalote**
leek	**un poireau**	spinach	**des épinards**
lettuce	**une laitue**	tomato	**une tomate**

Fish, meat and fowl

beef	**du bœuf**	lamb	**de l'agneau**
chicken	**du poulet**	plaice	**du carrelet**
duck	**du canard**	pork	**du porc**
fish	**du poisson**	salmon	**du saumon**
goose	**de l'oie**	sole	**de la sole**
haddock	**de l'aiglefin**	trout	**de la truite**
ham	**du jambon**	turkey	**de la dinde**

Groceries

biscuits	**des (biscuits/ petits gâteaux)**
bread	**du pain**
butter	**du beurre**
cake	**un gâteau**
goat's cheese	**du fromage de chèvre**
chocolate	**du chocolat**
coffee	**du café**
eggs	**des œufs**
frozen food	**des surgelés**
fruit juice	**un jus de fruit**

jam	**de la confiture**	rice	**le riz**
marmalade	**de la marmelade d'orange**	salt	**le sel**
		soup	**la soupe**
milk	**du lait**	sugar	**du sucre**
mustard	**de la moutarde**	tea	**du thé**
(olive) oil	**de l'huile (d'olive)**	tinned food	**les boîtes de conserve**
pasta	**les pâtes**	vinegar	**le vinaigre**
pepper	**le poivre**	yoghurt	**un yaourt**

Delicatessen

takeaway dishes	**les plats à emporter**
vegetarian dishes	**les plats végétariens**
knuckle of ham	**un jambonneau**
cured ham	**du jambon de Bayonne**
pig's trotters	**des pieds de porc**
cold, slicing sausage	**du saucisson**
garlic sausage	**du saucisson à l'ail**
tongue (veal/ox)	**de la langue (de veau/de bœuf)**
coarse pâté (of pork, duck, etc)	**des rillettes**
liver pâté	**du pâté de foie**
suckling pig	**un cochon de lait**
snails	**des escargots**
frogs' legs	**les cuisses de grenouille**

Bread

farmhouse bread	**un pain de campagne**
large French stick	**un pain restaurant**
long French stick	**une baguette**
narrower French stick	**une ficelle/une flûte**
rye bread	**un pain de seigle**
sandwich loaf	**un pain de mie**
wholemeal bread	**du pain (complet/bis)**

Pastries

apple tart	**une tarte aux pommes**
cream cake	**un gâteau à la crème**
cream vanilla-slice	**un mille-feuilles**
croissant	**un croissant**
rum baba	**un baba au rhum**
sweet bun	**une brioche**
yule log	**une bûche de Noël**

Sweets

almond sweets	**les calissons d'Aix**	lollipop	**une sucette**
crystallised chestnuts	**les marrons glacés**	marzipan-stuffed dates	**les dattes fourrées**
crystallised fruit	**les fruits confits**	soft toffee	**un caramel mou**
		sugared almonds	**des dragées**

tirez

poussez

push

Clothes shopping

I'm just looking, thanks.	**Je regarde seulement, merci.**
I'd like a skirt.	**Je voudrais une jupe.**
in (wool/cotton/silk/leather)	**en (laine/coton/soie/cuir)**
I'm a size 12.	**Je fais du 40.**
Can I try it on?	**Je peux l'essayer?**
It's too (tight/large).	**C'est trop (serré/grand).**
Do you have anything smaller?	**Vous en avez un/e plus petit/e?**
Do you have the same in yellow?	**Avez-vous le même en jaune?**
I (like/don't like) it.	**Ça (me plaît/ne me plaît pas).**
It (fits/doesn't fit).	**Ça (me va/ne me va pas).**
I'll take it.	**Je le prends.**
I'll think about it.	**Je vais réfléchir.**

Quelle (taille/pointure)?	What (size/shoe size)?
Quelle couleur?	What colour do you want?
Ça vous plaît?	Do you like it?

belt	**une ceinture**	shoes	**des chaussures**
bikini	**un bikini**	skirt	**une jupe**
blouse	**un corsage**	socks	**des chaussettes**
coat	**un manteau**		
dress	**une robe**	short-sleeved	**à manches courtes**
jumper	**un pull**		
long-sleeved	**à manches longues**	swimming costume	**un maillot (de bain)**
night dress	**une chemise de nuit**	tie	**une cravate**
		tights	**un pantalon**
shirt	**une chemise**	trousers	**un collant**

At the department store

Where's the . . . department?	**Où est le rayon de . . . ?**
Where can I find perfume?	**Où sont les parfums?**
Is there an escalator?	**Il y a un escalier roulant?**

Au sous-sol.	In the basement.
Au rez-de-chaussée.	On the ground floor
Au (premier/ deuxième) étage.	On the (first/ second) floor.
jouets	toys
parfums/produits de beauté	perfumes/beauty products
quincaillerie	hardware
sports	sports
vêtements enfants/femmes/ hommes	children's/women /men's clothes

Household goods

battery	**une pile**	razor blades	**des lames de rasoir**
bleach	**de l'eau de Javel**		
corkscrew	**un tire-bouchon**	sanitary towels	**des serviettes hygiéniques**
insect repellent	**un insecticide**		
light bulb	**une ampoule**	shampoo	**du shampoing**
matches	**des allumettes**	soap	**du savon**
nappies	**des couches**	toilet paper	**du papier hygiénique**
paper	**des mouchoirs**		
hankies	**en papier**	washing powder	**de la lessive**
plasters	**des pansements adhésifs**	washing-up liquid	**du liquide pour la vaisselle**

Buying stamps and newspapers

How much is a stamp to England?
for (a letter/a postcard)
Un timbre pour l'Angleterre, c'est combien?
pour (une lettre/une carte postale)

Three (4 francs 60) stamps, please.
Trois timbres (à quatre francs soixante), s'il vous plaît.

I'd like to send this to Australia.
Je voudrais envoyer ça en Australie.

Do you have any English newspapers?
Vous avez des journaux anglais?

Photography

A 35mm film (for prints/slides), please.
Une pellicule trente-cinq millimètres pour (photos papier/diapositives), s'il vous plaît.

Can you develop this?
Pouvez-vous développer ça?

(matt/glossy) finish
mat/brillant

When will it be ready?
Ça sera prêt quand?

(Aujourd'hui/Demain).
(Today/Tomorrow).

Dans (une heure/trois heures).
In (one hour/three hours).

Voulez-vous des doubles?
Do you want copies?

Souvenirs and gifts

bag	**un sac**
bottle of perfume	**un flacon de parfum**
brooch	**une broche**
earrings	**des boucles d'oreille**
keyring	**un porte-clés**
lace	**de la dentelle**
leather goods	**de la maroquinerie**
purse	**un porte-monnaie**
scarf	**un foulard**
wallet	**un portefeuille**

Sound Check

r
r is always scraped in the back of the throat. Make the back of your tongue touch the roof of your mouth and breathe.

beurre	bur
voudrais	voudray
traveller's	travellers
boucherie	bousheree

Practise on these words:
pharmacie, grammes, mandarine

Language works

Buying food

pissaladière

1 Buying sandwich fillings
- Bonjour, je peux vous aider?
- □ Le Roquefort, c'est combien?
- Cent quarante francs le kilo.
- □ Deux cents grammes, s'il vous plaît.
- Voilà. Autre chose?
- □ Quatre tranches de saucisson à l'ail, six tranches de jambon et une plaquette de beurre.

Roquefort costs . . . a kilo.

2 Buying some fruit for a picnic a a market
- Bonjour Mademoiselle, avez-vous des cerises?
- □ Désolée, il n'en reste plus . . . des fraises?
- C'est combien, les fraises?
- □ Quarante francs le kilo.
- Un demi-kilo, s'il vous plaît.
- □ Voilà les fraises. Autre chose?
- Six bananes . . . C'est tout. Ça fait combien?

The trader offers cherries/strawberri

Clothes shopping

3 Looking for the right size
- Je peux essayer ce pantalon?
- □ Oui. Là-bas.
- Taille quarante-quatre, c'est tro grand. Vous en avez un plus peti
- □ Voilà. Quarante-deux.
- . . . Ah bon! Ça me va! Avez-vous le même en bleu ou en vert?
- □ Oui, le voilà en bleu.
- Bon, ça me plaît. Je le prends. Je peux payer avec ma carte de crédit?

(**Là-bas** = over there)

They did/didn't have any blue trouse left.

At the department store

4 Asking where various departments are
- Excusez-moi, Mademoiselle, où sont les produits de beauté?
- □ Au sous-sol, Madame.
- Et le rayon des sports?
- □ Au deuxième étage.

The sports department is on the second/third floor.

Buying stamps

Enquiring about stamps at a
obacconist's
Vous vendez des timbres?
Oui, Madame. Pour la France?
**Non, pour l'Angleterre. Un timbre
pour une carte postale, c'est
combien?**
Quatre francs.
**Bon. Six timbres à quatre francs,
s'il vous plaît.**

ne stamp costs . . .

Photography

6 Buying and developing a film
■ **Bonjour Monsieur, pouvez-vous
développer ça?**
□ **Bien sûr. Voulez-vous des
doubles?**
■ **Non, merci. Ça sera prêt quand?**
□ **Dans trois heures ou demain?**
■ **Demain, s'il vous plaît.**

Could the photos have been
developed quicker?

Try it out

Match up

Match the souvenirs with the
relevant department
1 **un corsage en dentelle**
2 **une ampoule**
3 **un paquet de mouchoirs**
4 **un flacon de parfum**

a **Parfumerie**
b **Vêtements-femmes**
c **Quincaillerie**
d **Produits de beauté– Pharmacie**

As if you were there

Asking for a pastry at the cake
shop
■ **Bonjour, je peux vous aider?**
□ (Say hello, I'd like that and ask
what it is)
■ **C'est une tarte aux pommes.**
□ (Say good and ask for another
one. Ask how much it is)

Café life

Cafés, brasseries and bars with pavement terraces and infinite opening hours are a part of French daily life. You'll find snacks and light lunches served throughout most of the day; alcohol and soft drinks from 7am to 1am. Drinks are expensive on the terrace, cheaper at the bar. Measures and prices are shown on the price list (*tarifs des consommations*) at the bar. On the terrace, be patient – your highly professional waiter has seen you; anyone in a hurry should drink at the bar. Pay your waiter (he will bring the bill on a saucer with your order, give change, tear a notch in the slip and leave it on the table). Alternatively, leave the right money (plus a small tip) in the saucer, or take the saucer and bill to the bar.

What's available to eat and when

7 am to 11.30 am coffee, tea, pastries (the latter before c.10am). Set breakfast (*petit-déjeuner complet*) may include juice, hot drinks and croissants or bread, butter and jam (*tartines*). Regulars tipple at the bar (*au comptoir*) from around 10 am.

By 11.30 tables are set for lunch: steak or tripe sausage (*andouillettes*) and chips (*frites*), omelettes, mixed salads (*salades composées*), daily special (*plats du jour*). Fixed-price menus offe good value. Ice cream, crème caramel, chocolate mousse, fruit tarts or meringue and custard (*île flottante*) are favourite desserts.

From 2 pm to around 5.30 pm snacks are available: small pizzas, toasted cheese sandwich (*croque-monsieur*), toasted cheese and egg sandwich (*croque-madame*), ice-cream

What sandwiches do you have
Quels sandwichs avez-vous?

Drinks

Pastis (south-east) Aniseed-and-herb apéritif taken with water (turns milky).
Kir Still or sparkling white wine with blackcurrant (*cassis*), strawberry (*fraise*) or raspberr (*framboise*) liqueur.
Sweet apéritif wines *Muscat de Rivesaltes, Banyuls* (from western Mediterranean coast); *Frontignan* (Montpellier area) *Pineau des Charentes* (red or white, from central Atlantic coast).
Eaux de vie Fruit liqueurs (usually *digestifs*). Try *kirsch*

AFE DE FLORE

(Alpine cherry liqueur), *genièvres* (juniper-based, from around Calais); various noted liqueurs from Limousin. Calvados (Normandy's cider liqueur) is drunk anytime with coffee (*un café-calva*). Chartreuse, the green herb liqueur from Voiron, near Lyon, is delicious straight, with tonic, or with hot chocolate *après-ski*.

Sweet sparkling wines Popular alternatives to champagne: *Clairette de Die, Crémant d'Alsace, Blanquette de Limoux, Crémant du Jura, Perlé de Groseille*.

Wine (see also p57) Expect huge restaurant mark-ups on bottled wine. In wine regions, try the house *carafe* (or *pichet*): often a cheaper, decent appellation or *vin de pays* from a local *cave coopérative*.

Beers Always *blonde* (i.e. lager) unless *brune* is specified. '*Un seize*' produces the favourite 'Kronenbourg 1664' anywhere. Other brews are Adelscott, Pelforth (*blonde* or *brune*) and the (big) bottled beers from the north *3 Monts* and *L'Angelus*.

Citron pressé/orange pressée
Freshly-squeezed lemon or orange juice on ice, with a jug of water.

Sirops Fruit or mint cordial, served as above (*menthe, cassis* etc, *à l'eau*).

Mineral water Springs such as Evian, Volvic, Perrier are world-famous. Ask for *non-gazeuse* (still) or *gazeuse* (sparkling). Connoisseurs should try naturally-sparkling varieties such as Vittel and Badoit.

I'd like a freshly squeezed lemon drink.
Je voudrais un citron pressé.

Phrasemaker

Asking what there is

Do you have any apple juice?	**Avez-vous du jus de pomme?**
What do you have (to drink/ to eat)?	**Qu'est-ce qu'il y a (à manger/ à boire)?**
What ice-creams do you have?	**Quelles glaces avez-vous?**
What's in it?	**Qu'est-ce qu'il y a dedans?**

Vous désirez?	What would you like?
Désolé, il n'en reste plus.	I'm sorry, we've run out.
Il y a (du jambon/ des moules).	There is/are (ham/mussels).

Ordering

I'd like a cheese sandwich.	**Je voudrais un sandwich au fromag**
Another one.	**Un/e autre.**
(With/without) butter/cream.	**(Avec/sans) beurre/crème.**

Avec (des glaçons/du citron)?	With (ice/lemon)?
Gazeuse ou non-gazeuse?	Fizzy or still?
Lequel?	Which one?
Payez à la caisse, s'il vous plaît.	Please pay at the till.
C'est un self-service.	It's self-service.
Quel parfum?	Which flavour (ice- cream)?
Tout de suite!	Right away!

Other useful phrases

Where are the toilets, please?	**Où sont les toilettes, s'il vous plaît**
Is there a telephone?	**Il y a un téléphone?**
Is service included?	**Le service est compris?**

Service (non-compris/en sus).	Service (not included/extra).
Le service est à la discrétion de la clientèle.	Service is at the customer's discretion.

Containers

ashtray	**un cendrier**	dish for fruit or ice-cream	**une coupe**
(half) bottle	**une (demi-) bouteille**	(small) glass	**un (petit) verre**
carafe	**une carafe**	half a pint	**un demi (25cl)**
(large) cup	**une (grande) tasse**	jug	**un pot**
		straw	**une paille**

Alcoholic drinks

aniseed-flavoured drink	**une anisette/ un Pastis/un Pernod/un Ricard**	(dry/sweet) white wine	**du vin blanc (sec/doux)**
aperitif	**un apéritif**	gin and tonic	**un gin-tonic**
apple brandy	**un calva(dos)**	kirsch	**un kirsch**
beer (draught/ bottled)	**une bière (pression/en bouteille)**	lager	**une (bière) blonde**
		plum brandy	**une mirabelle**
blackcurrant liqueur	**un cassis**	port	**un porto**
		red wine	**du vin rouge**
brandy	**un cognac**	rosé wine	**du vin rosé**
champagne	**du champagne**	shandy	**un panaché**
cider	**un cidre**	sparkling wine	**du vin mousseux**
dark beer	**une (bière) brune**	vodka	**une vodka**
		whisky	**un whisky**
		white wine and blackcurrant liqueur	**un kir**

Hot drinks

coffee with cream	**un (café) crème**	fruit tea	**une tisane**
milky coffee	**un café au lait**	cocoa	**un cacao**
small shot of black coffee	**un café**	hot chocolate	**un chocolat chaud**
an expresso	**un express**		
weak black coffee	**un café léger**		
filtered coffee	**un café filtre**		
decaffeinated coffee	**un décaféiné**		
tea with milk/ lemon	**un thé au (lait/ citron)**		
tea without milk	**un thé nature**		
herbal tea	**une infusion**		
mint tea	**un thé à la menthe**		

Soft drinks

soft drinks	**boissons sans alcool**	fizzy mineral water	**de l'eau minérale gazeuse**
freshly squeezed lemon	**un citron pressé**	soda water	**de l'eau de Seltz**
fruit juice	**un jus de fruits**	still mineral water	**de l'eau minérale non gazeuse**
(diet) coke	**un coca (sans sucre)**	tonic water	**un Schweppes**
fizzy orange	**une orangeade**	alcohol-free beer	**une bière sans alcool**
fruit and lemonade cordial	**un diabolo**	iced coffee	**un café frappé**
lemonade	**une limonade**	milk	**du lait**
mint and lemonade cordial	**un diabolo-menthe**	milkshake	**un milkshake**

crêpe

croque-monsieur

Snacks

(cheese/ham) sandwich	**un sandwich (au fromage/au jambon)**
ham salad sandwich	**un américain**
toasted sandwich with ham and melted cheese	**un croque-monsieur**
toasted sandwich with ham, melted cheese and a fried egg	**un croque-madame**
(plain/mixed herbs) omelette	**une omelette (nature/fines herbes)**
(mussels/steak) and chips	**un (moules/steak)-frites**
mixed salad of tuna, tomatoes, anchovies and olives	**une salade niçoise**
(apple) fritters	**les beignets (aux pommes)**
continental breakfast	**un café complet**
pancake	**une crêpe**
waffles	**les gaufres**

les glaces

Ice-creams

ice-creams	**les glaces (f)**
choc-ice on stick	**un esquimau**
cornet	**un cornet**
ice lolly made with fruit	**une sucette glacée**
iced coffee topped with whipped cream	**un café liégeois**
ice-cream (strawberry/pistachio/chocolate)	**une glace (à la fraise/à la pistache/au chocolat)**
tub	**une barquette**
wafer	**une gaufrette**
mixed water ice (vanilla-lemon)	**un panaché (vanille-citron)**

Sound Check

s, added to the end of a noun to make it plural, is not pronounced

une paille	ewn paye
deux pailles	duh paye
un sandwich	uh sawndweech
deux sandwichs	duh sawndweech

Practise on these words: **deux glaces, deux thés**

Language works

Drinks

1 Ordering for several people
- **Bonjour, Messieurs Dames, vous désirez?**
- □ **Bonjour, un grand crème, une blonde, un verre de vin et un citron pressé, s'il vous plaît.**
- **Vin blanc, rouge ou rosé?**
- □ **Vin blanc, s'il vous plaît.**
- **Bien, tout de suite.**
  The waiter comes back with the drinks:
  Voilà, Messieurs Dames.
- □ **Merci. Ça fait combien?**

The waiter suggests . . . , . . . or . . . wine.

Try it out

As if you were there

Ordering drinks and snacks

- **Bonjour Messieurs Dames.**
- □ (Ask for a freshly squeezed lemon drink without ice, a tea with milk and a glass of white wine)
- **Autre chose?**
- □ (Ask what sandwiches they have)
- **Fromage, jambon, américain.**
- □ (Ask for a ham salad sandwich and some chocolate ice-cream)
- **Bien, tout de suite.**

Odd one out

Find the item in each list which does not fit in.
1 une crêpe, un américain, un croque-madame, un jus de raisin, du saucisson.
2 une blonde, un grand crème, un vin rouge, une glace au chocolat, un chocolat chaud.

Eating out

Where to eat

Restaurants and **bistrots** open from around 11.30am – 2.30pm and roughly 7.30pm – 10.15pm (last orders – you're never hassled to leave). Some specialise in fish and seafood (*poissons* and *fruits de mer*) or grills with a choice of sauces (*grillades*). Colonial cuisines include North African *couscous* and Vietnamese, Caribbean, Corsican, Tahitian or Réunionais (French Indian Ocean). Variously-priced all-inclusive menus are posted outside. *Formules express/ repas d'affaires* (business specials) offer a main course plus starter or sweet and wine.

Chambres d'hôte and fermes-auberges may serve dinner – often great French home cooking.

Brasseries café-style drinking establishments, serving more substantial meals. Open from morning till late.

Crêperies (licensed) open from lunch till late, serving savoury and sweet pancakes, salads etc.

Pizzerias keep similar hours. Look for wood-fired ovens (*au feu de bois*).

Salons de thé (tearooms) open from around 9 am to 7 pm, serving pastries, sandwiches and light lunches (quiches, salads).

Vegetarians may fare best in *crêperies*, pizzerias or *salons de thé*. In restaurants and cafés, try mixed salads (*salades composées*) or omelettes but check for those sneaky bacon bits (*lardons*). Try *soupe au pistou* or ratatouille (see Menu reader, p80).

❗ A table for two, non-smoking, please.
⬤ **Une table pour deux personnes, non-fumeur, s'il vous plaît.**

bouillabaisse

What to try

A full-scale French meal can have six courses: *apéritifs*, starters (*entrées*), fish, a main course (*le plat*), salad, cheese and dessert. Top-price set menus may feature all six; others skip the fish, and offer salad with cheese, or cheese or dessert. Smart places may serve sorbet and eau de vie (*le trou normand*) after the fish. Wines and *digestifs* are integral to the meal, but not always included in the price. Service is included.

A simpler alternative is a meal-in-one (*un plat unique*) – often a menu option for two or more (individual portions may be available):

Aïoli (Provence) Garlicky olive oil mayonnaise with salted cod, seafood and carrots, potatoes, courgettes. . .

Bouillabaisse (Marseille) Mediterranean fish and seafood with olive oil, tomatoes and saffron, scalded and boiled briefly but furiously. Served with toasted bread and pepper paste (*rouille*).

Cassoulet (the south-west) Chunky pork sausages, preserved goose or duck (*confit*) and white haricot beans baked in goose fat in an earthenware pot. Castelnaudary is France's *cassoulet* capital.

Choucroute (Alsace) Preserved cabbage, gammon, smoked bacon joints and sausages baked in white

cassoulet

wine (Riesling or Sylvaner) with cloves and juniper berries.

Couscous (a North African import): *Couscous royale* features spicy lamb sausage (*merguez*), chicken and lamb in a broth of chick peas, carrots, tomatoes etc. Bulgar wheat (*semoule*) is steamed over the pot. Spoon on the fiery *harissa* sauce at your own risk.

Plateau de fruits de mer (Brittany) Lobster, langoustines, oysters, mussels, cockles, clams, small crabs and prawns, with bread (wholemeal/rye) and mayonnaise.

Soupe au pistou (Provence) Three-bean stew with *pistou* (ground pine nuts, parmesan, garlic, olive oil) and *pain de campagne*.

Raclette (Savoy Alps) Potatoes and ham, salamis (*charcuterie*) draped in melted raclette cheese.

! Do you do children's portions?
Vous faites des portions-enfants?

raclette cheese

Phrasemaker

Finding somewhere to eat

Is there a good (little) restaurant near by?	**Il y a un bon (petit) restaurant dans le quartier?**

Tableware

ashtray	**un cendrier**	oil and vinegar cruet	**l'huilier**
breadbasket	**la corbeille à pain**	pepper	**du poivre**
cup	**une tasse**	place setting	**le couvert**
fork	**une fourchette**	small plate	**une petite assiette**
glass	**un verre**	salt	**du sel**
fish-knife	**un couteau à poisson**	(soup/dessert) spoon	**une cuillère (à soupe/ à dessert)**
matches	**des allumettes**		
mustard cruet	**la moutarde**	tablecloth	**la nappe**
napkin	**une serviette**	toothpicks	**des cure-dents**

Arriving

A table for two, non-smoking.	**Une table pour deux personnes, non-fumeur.**
I'd like to reserve a table for four people, for this evening.	**Je voudrais réserver une table pour quatre personnes, pour ce soir.**

Asking about the menu

The menu, please.	**La carte, s'il vous plaît.**
Is there a menu of the day?	**Il y a un menu du jour?**
Have you got . . . ?	**Avez-vous . . . ?**
What do you recommend?	**Qu'est-ce que vous recommandez?**
What's the local speciality?	**Quelle est la spécialité régionale?**
What's this?	**Qu'est-ce que c'est?**
Is it (strong/spicy)?	**C'est (fort/épicé)?**

Vous désirez?	What would you like?
Vous voulez commander?	Are you ready to order?
Aujourd'hui, nous avons . . .	Today, we have . . .
C'est (un gros poisson/une sorte de champignon).	It's (a large fish/a type of mushroom).
Désolé/e, nous n'avons pas de . . .	Sorry, we haven't got any . . .

Ordering

I'll have (this/the 140 francs menu).	Je prends (ça/le menu à cent quarante francs).
as a (starter/main course/side dish)	comme (hors d'œuvre/plat principal/d'accompagnement)
Does it come with vegetables?	C'est garni?
Do you do children's portions?	Vous faites des portions-enfants?
No (dessert/coffee).	Pas de (dessert/café).

Comment vous le voulez?	How would you like it cooked?
Vous désirez un dessert?	Would you like a dessert?
Comme boisson?	Anything to drink?
Le service (est/n'est pas) compris.	Service (is/isn't) included.
Service en sus.	Service is extra.
Ça vous plaît?	Do you like it?
Bon appétit!	Enjoy your meal!

Eating preferences

I'm allergic to . . .	**Je suis allergique à . . .**
I'm (vegetarian/vegan) (male).	**Je suis (végétarien/végétalien).**
I'm (vegetarian/vegan) (female).	**Je suis (végétarienne/végétalienne).**
Has it got (meat/nuts) in it?	**Il y a (de la viande/des noix) dedans?**

Drinks

(See pp88–89 for more drinks.)

restaurant on the Champs-Élysées, Paris

The drinks list, please.	**La carte des boissons, s'il vous plaît.**
a (half) bottle of wine	**une (demi-) bouteille de vin**
house wine	**la réserve du patron**
a beer	**une bière**
(fizzy/still) water	**de l'eau (gazeuse/non gazeuse)**
mineral water	**de l'eau minérale**
tap water	**de l'eau du robinet**

During the meal

Excuse me! (Waiter!)	**(Monsieur/Mademoiselle!), s'il vous plaît!**
Where is my meal?	**Est-ce que ça vient?**
I've been waiting half an hour!	**J'attends depuis une demi-heure!**
I didn't order (this/the pudding).	**Je n'ai pas commandé (ça/ le dessert).**
Another (beer/bottle of . . .).	**Une autre (bière/bouteille de . . .)**
More bread, please.	**Encore du pain, s'il vous plaît.**
It's (delicious/very good).	**C'est (délicieux/très bon).**
It's (cold/under done/tough).	**C'est (froid/pas assez cuit/dur).**
Where are the toilets?	**Où sont les toilettes?**
(Cette tarte/cette grillade) est pour qui?	Who is (this tart/this grilled meat) for?
(Monsieur/Madame) est satisfait/e?	Everything all right, (Sir/ Madam)?
Vous désirez autre chose/ Autre chose?	Anything else?

Paying

truffes

The bill, please.	**L'addition, s'il vous plaît.**
Do you take credit cards?	**Vous acceptez les cartes de crédit?**
Is service included?	**Le service est compris?**
There's a mistake, I think.	**Il y a une erreur, je crois.**
We didn't have (any beer/ two desserts).	**Nous n'avons pas pris (une bière/deux desserts).**

Language works

Ordering a meal

1 Choosing and ordering a set menu for one
- **Bonsoir, Monsieur.**
- □ **Il y a un menu du jour?**
- □ **Oui, voilà, Monsieur: un menu à cent quarante francs et un menu à cent vingt francs . . .**
- □ **Bon. Je prends le menu à cent vingt francs.**
- **Et comme boisson?**
- **Qu'est-ce que vous recommandez? Un vin rosé?**
- **La réserve du patron est excellente. C'est un vin du pays.**
- □ **Bon! Une demi-bouteille de rosé, s'il vous plaît.**

The waiter recommends . . .

2 Asking about a particular dish
- **Alors . . . Vous voulez commander, Madame?**
- □ **Oui, s'il vous plaît. Qu'est-ce que c'est la bouillabaisse?**
- **C'est une soupe de poissons; c'est une spécialité régionale.**
- □ **Oh! Je suis végétarienne!**
- **Aujourd'hui, nous avons du couscous aux légumes. C'est délicieux!**
- □ **Bon, je prends ça.**

The waitress suggests . . . .

Try it out

Jumbled-up menu

Use the Menu reader to find out which dish goes under which heading
1 Meat   4 Seafood
2 Fowl   5 Vegetarian
3 Fish   6 Desserts

a bifteck-frites
b sole meunière
c ratatouille
d moules marinière
e banane flambée
f poulet au riz

As if you were there

Order from a set menu and choose a drink
- **Vous voulez commander?**
- □ (Say you'll have artichoke as a starter and mussels as the main dish. Ask if it's served with vegetables)
- **Oui: pommes allumettes.**
- □ (Ask for a green salad as a side dish)
- **Très bien. Et comme boisson?**
- □ (Ask for a glass of white wine)
- **Tout de suite, Monsieur.**

Sound Check

ill is usually pronounced as a 'y' sound, like 'y' in 'yet'.
| **fille** | feey |
| **oreille** | oraye |

also
| **appareil-photo** | apparaye-foto |

but there are some exceptions to this rule:
| **ville** | veel |
| **village** | vee-aj |

Menu Reader

Courses

hors d'œuvres/entrées starters
spécialités specialities
légumes vegetables
viandes meat dishes
volailles, gibier, venaison fowl, game, venison
plats de poissons, fruits de mer,

crustacés fish, sea food, shell fish dishes
(plateau de) fromages cheese (platter)
entremets/desserts desserts
pâtisseries choice of cakes
gâteaux cakes

Main ways of cooking

à l'ancienne according to a traditional recipe
aigre-doux sweet and sour
au bleu cooked in water, white wine and herbs
bien cuit well cooked (steak)
bleu very rare (steak)
bouilli boiled
à la broche spit-roasted
brouillé scrambled (egg)
de campagne country style
cru raw
émincé cut into thin strips and served in a sauce
en cocotte casseroled
en croûte covered with pastry
en daube casseroled (with wine)
en gelée in aspic/jellied
farci stuffed
flambé brandy poured on food and set alight briefly
au four baked
fricassé stewed
frit fried
fumé smoked
garni served with vegetables

glacé crystallised
goujonnade in narrow strips (usually refers to fish)
gratiné melted cheese on top
grillé grilled
hâché minced
jardinière with mixed vegetables
maison/du chef homemade
mariné marinated
meunière dipped in flour and fried in butter, with lemon juice and parsley
à la normande in a cream based sauce
pané fried in breadcrumbs
poché poached
à point medium cooked (steak)
à la provençale with tomatoes, onions, garlic and herbs
au pot stewed
râpé grated
rôti roast
saignant rare (steak)
sauté stir-fried
sur le plat fried (egg)
vapeur steamed

Picnic treats

aucisson or **cervelas** two tasty
pes of cold, sliced sausages.

oubressade a fairly spicy, very
oft, red sausage meat which is
est spread with butter on French
read.

omages French cheeses have
ery different textures and tastes.
ook out for *Brie*, *Camembert*,
Gruyère but also all sorts of
goat's cheese *Fromage de
chèvre*.

marrons glacés crystallised
chestnuts which should be moist.
Expensive but delicious!

dattes fourrées dates stuffed
with (usually green) marzipan.

Cakes and pastries from the *pâtisserie*

ioche a soft, sweet, golden bun
ade with egg and milk.

oissant a crescent-shaped,
aky pastry especially delicious
ten warm with a little jam.

**etit pain (au chocolat/aux
isins)** a soft roll, made with
ilk, which contains chocolate or
isins.

lette des Rois this almond-
avoured Epiphany cake hides a
tle figurine or broadbean (*fève*).
hoever finds the *fève* is King or
ueen for the day. Available in
nuary and early February.

tartes aux fraises

The menu

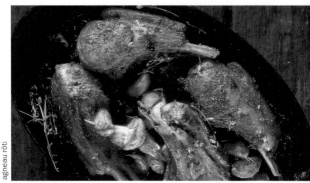

agneau rôti

abricot apricots
agneau lamb
aiglefin haddock
ail garlic
aïoli garlic mayonnaise
airelles cranberries
amandes almonds
ananas pineapple
anchois anchovies
andouille(tte) (small) chitterling sausage
anguille eel
artichaut globe artichoke
   à la barigoule braised, stuffed artichoke
asperges asparagus
assiette de plate of
assiette anglaise assorted, cold, roast meats
aubergine aubergine/egg plant
avocat avocado
baeckeoffe mixed meat and vegetable casserole (Alsace)
banane banana
bar bass
barquette small boat-shaped pastry/punnet
basilic basil
bâtonnets de crabe crab sticks
bavaroise type of light mousse
bavette à l'échalote beef with shallots

béarnaise butter, egg yolk, shallot, vinegar and herb sauce
bécasse woodcock
béchamel white sauce
beignet doughnut/fritter
belon belon oyster
bercy butter, white wine and shallot sauce
betterave beetroot
beurre butter
   blanc white butter sauce with white wine and vinegar
   maître d'hôtel parsley butter
   noir browned butter sauce
bifteck beefsteak
   tartare raw steak minced with raw egg, onion and Worcester sauce
bigarade brown sauce with oranges
bigorneaux winkles
bijoux choux pastries (Provence)
biscuit de Savoie sponge cake
bisque rich, shellfish soup
blanchaille whitebait
blanquette de veau veal stew in lemon and white sauce
bœuf beef
   à la mode braised beef with red wine and vegetables
   bourguignon beef cooked

in red wine and mushrooms
en daube beef braised in red wine and herbs
miroton beef stewed with onions
olets boletus mushrooms
ouchée à la reine chicken vol-au-ent
oudin (blanc/noir) (white/black) udding

boudin noir

ouillabaisse chunky mixed fish oup (Marseille)
ouillon broth
oulettes meatballs
ouquet rose prawn
ourride fish stew with garlic ayonnaise
raisé braised
randade de morue salted cod eamed with potato
rochet pike
rochette kebab
rugnon nectarine
abillaud cod
abri kid
acahuètes peanuts
aille quail
almar/calamar squid
anard duck
  sauvage wild duck
aneton duckling
annelle cinnamon
âpres capers
arbonnade de boeuf beef stewed beer with onions
arottes carrots

Vichy boiled/glazed carrots with butter and sugar
carpe carp
carré d'(agneau) loin of (lamb)
carrelet plaice
cassis blackcurrant/s
cassoulet casserole of haricot beans, mutton, pork, goose and sausage (Toulouse)
céleri celery
céleri-rave celeriac
cèpes boletus mushrooms
cerises cherries
cervelas saveloy (a seasoned, smoked, red pork sausage)
cervelle brains
champignons mushrooms
  à la grecque mushrooms in olive oil, herbs and tomato sauce
charcuterie assorted, cooked, cold, pork meats
charlotte creamy, fruit filling in a sponge or bread case
châteaubriand large fillet steak
chausson aux pommes apple turn-over
chevreuil venison
chicorée endive
chips crisps
chocolat chocolate
(au) choix choice/to choose from
chou cabbage
chou-fleur cauliflower
chou frisé kale
chou-navet swede/rutabaga
chou-rave kohlrabi
chou rouge red cabbage
choucroute garnie sauerkraut served with smoked ham, sausages and potatoes
chouquette sugar bun
choux à la crème cream puffs
choux de Bruxelles Brussel sprouts
ciboulettes chives
citron lemon
civet de (lapin/lièvre) jugged (rabbit/hare) (stewed)

clafoutis

clafoutis fruit cooked in batter
cochon de lait sucking pig
cœurs d'artichaut globe artichoke hearts
coing quince
colin hake
compote stewed fruit
concombre cucumber
confit d'oie goose preserved in fat
confiture jam
consommé clear soup
contre-filet sirloin
coq au vin chicken in red wine, bacon, onion and mushroom sauce
coquilles St-Jacques scallops served in their shells, in a cream sauce
corbeille basket
cornichon gherkin
côte rib
côtelette cutlet/chop
coulis purée-like sauce
coupe de fruits fruit salad
coupe glacée ice-cream sundae
courgette courgette/zucchini
court-bouillon stock
couscous steamed semolina served with meat and vegetables
crabe crab
à la crème in a cream sauce
crème cream/cream soup
  anglaise custard
  brûlée/caramel fresh caramel custard
  chantilly whipped cream

  dubarry cream of cauliflower soup
  pâtissière confectioner's custard
  renversée crème caramel
  vichyssoise cold cream of leek and potato soup made with chicken stock
crêpe pancake
  suzette pancake with orange or lemon sauce, flamed with brandy
cresson watercress
crevettes roses prawns
crevettes grises shrimps
croquembouche pile of caramel-coated choux pastry puffs
croque-madame toasted ham and cheese sandwich, with a fried egg
croque-monsieur toasted ham and cheese sandwich
croquettes de poisson fish finger
croustade pastry shell
crudités assorted raw vegetable with a vinaigrette dressing
cuisses de (grenouille) (frogs') legs
darne thick fish steak
dattes dates
daurade sea bream
désossé boned
à la diable devilled
dinde/dindon/dindonneau turkey
douzaine dozen
échalotes shallots
éclair finger-shaped choux pastry filled with cream
écrevisse crayfish
encornet squid
endive endive/chicory
entrecôte rib steak
épaule de shoulder of
épinards spinach
escalope escalope (boneless slice of meat)
  de veau milanaise breaded veal escalope with tomato sauce
escargots snails
  à la bourguignonne snails in garlic butter
estragon tarragon

faisan pheasant
faux-filet sirloin
fenouil fennel
féra type of fresh water salmon
fèves broad beans
figues figs
filet (mignon) (small) fillet
fines herbes mixed herbs
flageolets small kidney beans
flan custard tart or pie
flétan halibut
foie liver
    de volaille chicken liver
    gras goose or duck liver pâté
fondue fondue
    bourguignonne meat fondue
fouetté whipped
frais/fraîche fresh; chilled
fraises strawberries
framboises raspberries
(de) Frankfort frankfurter
frites chips
fromage cheese
    blanc soft cream cheese
    de chèvre goat's cheese
    demi-sel soft cream cheese, slightly salted
fruits de mer sea food
galantine cold poultry or game, in aspic or gelatine
galette pancake made with buckwheat flour/savoury pancake
gamba large prawn (Mediterranean)
garbure thick cabbage soup
gâteau gateau/cake
    Breton butter cake
    Paris-Brest large ring-shaped choux pastry
    aux marrons chestnut, chocolate and brandy cake
gaufre waffle/wafer
germes de soja bean sprouts
gibier game
gigot de leg of
gingembre ginger
girolle chanterelle mushroom
glace (à la fraise) (strawberry) ice-cream
goujon gudgeon/narrow strips

granité type of sorbet
gras-double tripe
gratin dauphinois sliced potatoes baked in cream
grenouille frog
griotte morello cherry
grive thrush
groseilles blanches white currants
groseilles rouges redcurrants
groseilles à maquereau gooseberries
hachis Parmentier shepherd's pie
hareng herring
hareng-saur marinated, cured herring fillet
haricot de mouton mutton stew with haricot beans
haricots beans
    blancs haricot beans
    rouges red kidney beans
    verts (French/green) beans

haricots verts

herbes herbs
homard lobster
    à l'américaine/à l'armoricaine lobster in wine, tomatoes, shallots and brandy
    Thermidor lobster in white wine, mushrooms, spices and flamed with brandy
hors d'œuvres (variés) (mixed) starters
huile oil
    d'arachide groundnut oil
    d'olive olive oil
    de tournesol sunflower oil
huîtres oysters
    chaudes oysters served warm with cream and chives

îles flottantes whisked egg whites floating in custard
jambon ham
  à l'os ham off the bone
  cru raw ham
  cuit cooked ham
  de Bayonne cured ham
  de Parme Parma ham
jarret knuckle/shin
du jour of the day
julienne soup of shredded vegetables
kugelhopf rich yeast cake with sultanas (Alsace)
laitue lettuce
langouste sea crayfish
langoustines scampi
langue tongue
lapin rabbit
  chasseur rabbit with white wine and herbs
lard streaky bacon/fat
lardons diced bacon
légumes vegetables
lentilles lentils
liégeois iced coffee with whipped cream
lièvre hare
limande lemon sole
longe loin
lotte burbot/monkfish
loup de mer sea bass
macédoine de fruits fruit salad
macédoine de légumes mixed vegetables
madeleine small shell-shaped sponge cake (often lemon-flavoured)
magret de (canard) breast of (duck)
maïs sweet corn
maquereau mackerel
marcassin young wild boar
marchand de vin red wine sauce with shallots
marmite dieppoise creamy, curry-flavoured mixed fish and seafood dish
marrons chestnuts
massepain marzipan
matelote fish stew

d'anguilles eel stew
médaillons tender loin steaks
melon melon
menthe mint
merguez spicy sausage
merlan whiting
merluche hake
miel honey
mille-feuilles vanilla cream slice
mojettes aux jambon haricot beans, ham and tomatoes
moka mocha cake (coffee flavoured)
morilles morel mushrooms
mortadelle Bologna sausage (a large, spiced, pork sausage)
morue cod
moules mussels
  marinière mussels cooked in their shells, in white wine, shallots and parsley

moules

mousse mousse
moutarde mustard
mouton mutton
mulet grey mullet
mûres blackberries
myrtilles bilberries/blueberries
nature/au naturel plain
navarin d'agneau lamb stew with vegetables
navet turnip
noisettes d'agneau small boneless rounds of lamb
noisettes hazelnuts
noix nuts/walnuts
  de coco coconut
  de pécan pecan nuts

ouilles noodles

euf/s egg/s

  à la coque soft-boiled egg

  brouillés scrambled egg

  dur hard-boiled egg

  dur mimosa stuffed, hard-boiled egg

  à la neige whisked egg white floating in custard

ie goose

ignon onion

lives olives

  farcies stuffed olives

  noires black olives

  vertes green olives

melette omelette

  norvégienne baked Alaska

  paysanne omelette with potatoes and bacon

nglet à l'échalote long, narrow teak fried with shallots

range orange

  givrée orange sorbet served in a scooped-out orange

seille sorrel

ursin sea urchin

ain bread

  d'épices gingerbread

alourdes clams

amplemousse grapefruit

anaché two flavours of ice-cream/shandy

an bagnat moist salad sandwich with tuna fish traditionally in a ound loaf or bun (Provence)

en) papillote baked in paper or oil

arfum (au choix) flavour

assé au four finished in the oven

astèque water melon

âtes pasta

âté pâté

  de campagne coarse pork pâté

  de foie liver pâté

âtisserie cakes

pauchoise fish stew (Burgundy)

paupiettes (de veau) rolled and stuffed slices (of veal)

peau skin

pêche peach

perche perch

perdrix partridge

persil parsley

petit pain roll/soft, sweet bun

petite friture whitebait

petits farcis stuffed vegetables

petits pois peas

pieds de porc pig's trotters

pigeon/pigeonneau pigeon

pintade guinea fowl

piperade tomatoes and sweet peppers served with scrambled eggs

pissaladière onion tart with black olives and anchovies

pissenlit aux lardons/vinaigrette warm dandelion salad with bacon/French dressing

gâteau au chocolat et pistache

pistache pistachio

plat/plateau (de fromages) dish/(cheese) board

plie plaice

pointes d'asperges asparagus tips

poire pear

  belle Hélène pear with vanilla ice-cream and chocolate sauce

poireaux leeks

pois chiches chickpeas

poisson fish

  au court-bouillon fish poached in aromatic stock

poitrine breast
poivre pepper
  noir black pepper
poivron vert green pepper
poivron jaune yellow pepper
poivron rouge red sweet pepper
pomme apple
  bonne femme baked apple
pomme de terre potatoes
  allumettes thin fried potatoes
  dauphine croquettes of potato
  mashed with butter and egg
  yolks and deep-fried
  duchesse potatoes mashed
  with butter and egg yolks
  en robe de chambre/des
  champs jacket potatoes
  mousseline/ purée mashed
  potatoes
  vapeur steamed potatoes
porc pork
pot-au-feu beef and vegetable
stew
potage thick vegetable soup
  bonne femme leek and potato
  soup
  Crécy carrot soup
  Parmentier potato soup
  printanier mixed vegetable
  soup
potée hotpot
poule hen, chicken
  au pot chicken poached with

vegetables
poulet chicken
  (à la) basquaise chicken
  basque-style, in a ham, tomato
  and pepper sauce
  au sang jugged chicken
  chasseur chicken in a wine,
  mushroom and tomato sauce
  frites chicken 'n' chips
  au riz chicken 'n' rice
  marengo chicken with white
  wine, tomatoes, garlic,
  mushrooms and shallots
poulpe octopus
poussin spring chicken
praline pieces of almond boiled in
sugar
profiteroles small choux pastry
puffs, filled with cream
prune plum
pruneau prune
purée (de) mashed
quenelle type of meat or fish
dumpling/semolina sausage
quetsches damson
queue de bœuf oxtail
quiche lorraine bacon, egg and
cheese flan
raclette hot melted cheese,
eaten with potatoes and pickles
(Switzerland)
radis radishes
ragoût meat stew/casserole
raie skate
raisin grapes
raisin sec raisins
rascasse scorpion fish (used in
bouillabaisse)
ratatouille vegetable stew of
courgettes, peppers, aubergines,
tomatoes and onions
reines-claudes greengages
religieuse chocolate or coffee
cream puff
rillettes (de porc/de saumon)
potted (pork/salmon)
ris de veau calf's sweetbreads
riz rice
  au lait rice pudding
rognons kidneys
romarin rosemary

poulet gasconne

rosbif roast beef
romsteck rump (beef)
rouget red mullet
   grillé sur feuilles de vigne red
   mullet barbecued on vine
   leaves (neither gutted nor
   scaled)
rouille spicy sauce made with
garlic, egg yolk, pepper and oil
roux sauce base made of flour
and browned butter
sablés rich shortbread biscuits
sabayon dessert of whipped egg
yolks with wine and sugar
saint-honoré gâteau of choux
pastry puffs and cream
saint-pierre John Dory fish
(de) saison in season

salade salad
   composée/mixte mixed salad
   de fruits rafraîchis fresh fruit
   salad
   niçoise tuna, tomato, anchovy
   and olive salad
   russe diced, cooked
   vegetables in mayonnaise
   verte green/lettuce salad
salmis game stew with wine and
vegetable sauce
salsifis salsify (a root vegetable)
sanglier wild boar
sans without
sauce sauce
   aurore white sauce with
   tomato purée
   béarnaise sauce made with
   butter, egg yolks, shallots,
   vinegar and herbs
   béchamel white sauce
   bercy butter sauce with white

wine and shallots
   bigarade brown sauce with
   oranges
   blanche white sauce
   bordelaise red wine,
   mushroom and shallot sauce
   chasseur white wine, shallots,
   tomatoes and mushrooms
   hollandaise egg yolks, butter
   and vinegar sauce
   mornay cheese sauce
   piquante hot, spicy sauce
   provençale tomato, garlic and
   herb sauce
   rémoulade mayonnaise with
   mustard and herbs
saucisse sausage
saucisson salami-style sausage
   sec dried sausage
saumon salmon
savarin type of rum baba cake
sel salt
selle de saddle of
sole sole
   bonne femme sole in white
   wine and mushrooms
sorbet sorbet

soufflés

soufflé soufflé
   Rothschild soufflé with
   candied fruits
soupe soup
   à l'oignon French onion soup,
   topped with cheese and bread
   au pistou thick potato,
   courgette, bean and herb soup
   (Provence)
   de pêcheurs Provence-style
   mixed fish soup

spaghetti spaghetti
stea(c)k steak
  au poivre steak with peppercorns
  frites steak 'n' chips
  haché minced meat
  tartare raw minced steak mixed with raw egg
sucre sugar
suprême de (volaille) (chicken) breast in a cream sauce
tapenade paste made with olives, anchovies, capers, mustard, garlic and lemon
tarte tart
  frangipane almond cream tart
  Tatin upside-down apple tart
tartelette small tart
tartine slice of bread and butter
terrine pâté
tête de veau calf's head

thon

thon tuna
timbales de ramekins of

tomates tomatoes
topinambour Jerusalem artichoke
tournedos thick fillet steak
  rossini thick fillet steak with foie gras and truffles, in a Madeira sauce
tourte layer cake/pie
tourteau au fromage cheesecake
tranche slice
travers spare rib
tripes tripe
  à la mode de Caen tripe cooked in cider, Calvados and herbs, served with vegetables
truffade mashed potatoes with cheese
truffe/truffé truffle/with truffles
truite trout
  au bleu poached trout
turbot turbot
vacherin (glacé) ice-cream and meringue gâteau
vanille vanilla
veau calf
velouté creamy soup
venaison venison
viande meat
vinaigre vinegar
vinaigrette French dressing
volaille poultry, chicken
waterzoi de poulet chicken in wine and cream sauce with vegetables
yaourt (plain) yoghurt (available as part of the cheese course)

The drinks

(see Café life, p66 for speciality drinks)

allongé diluted with hot water
apéritif aperitif
appellation d'origine contrôlée/ AOC guarantee of a wine's quality
armagnac brandy
bière beer
  anglaise English beer

  blonde lager
  brune dark beer
  en bouteille bottled beer
  pression draught beer
blanc de blancs white wine made from white grapes
bouteille de bottle of
cacao cocoa

café small cup of strong black coffee
  complet continental breakfast
  filtre filtered coffee
  frappé iced coffee
Calva(dos) apple brandy
carafe de carafe of
carte des vins wine list
cassis blackcurrant liqueur
champagne champagne
chocolat chaud hot chocolate
cidre cider
citron lemon
crème coffee with frothy milk/cream
cru vintage wine
décaféiné decaffeinated
demi draught beer (half pint)
doux/douce sweet
eau water
  de Seltz soda water
  minérale gazeuse fizzy mineral water
  minérale non gazeuse still mineral water
eau-de-vie brandy
express espresso
gin gin
gin-tonic gin and tonic
(grand) café (large) espresso
grand cru vintage wine
infusion herbal tea
jus juice
jus de fruit fruit juice
kir white wine and cassis
  royal champagne and cassis
kirsch kirsch
lait milk
léger weak (coffee)
limonade lemonade
menthe mint tea/peppermint cordial
milkshake milkshake
mirabelle plum brandy
muscat sweet fortified white wine
noisette strong black coffee with a tiny amount of milk added
orange orange
panaché shandy
Pastis aniseed-flavoured apéritif

petit crème small coffee with frothy milk or cream
pichet de jug of
porto port
premier cru vintage wine
pressé freshly-squeezed
pression draught beer
quetsche plum brandy
réserve du patron house wine
rhum rum
Ricard aniseed-flavoured aperitif
sans alcool alcohol-free
sans glaçons without ice
Schweppes tonic water
sec/sèche dry
serré extra-strong (coffee)
soda fizzy drink
thé tea
  à la menthe mint tea
  nature black tea
tilleul linden tea
tisane fruit tea
vermouth vermouth
verre glass
verveine verbena tea
vin wine
  blanc white wine
  cuit fortified wine
  de cru local wine
  de table table wine
  doux sweet wine
  du pays local wine
  du Rhin hock
  mousseux sparkling wine
  ordinaire table wine
  rosé rosé wine
  rouge red wine
vodka vodka
whisky whisky (and soda)
xérès sherry

kir, olives

Entertainment and leisure

Finding out what's on

Local *Offices de Tourisme* are the essential first call for hotels, restaurants, events and attractions. Many publish free listings. Away from tourist centres, look for the *Syndicat d'Initiative*.

Local listings magazines Free from venues and information offices, or sold in newsagents (Presse symbol).

Regional newspapers

English-language publications Cater for ex-pats, but can be useful for visitors. Try *The News* (Dordogne), *Riviera Reporter* (free from English bookshops on the Côte d'Azur), *Lyon Capitale* (weekly English page).

! Do you have any information in English?
● **Avez-vous des informations en anglais?**

Spectator Events

Music

Traditional accordion-playing will feature at any *bal populaire* (local dance), or the *Fête de la Musique* (free street music throughout France on June 21). Churches regularly host classical concerts (often free); jazz is much-loved, and big names frequently tour. Club venues are fast-changing – consult local listings. Listen out for French rap from the *banlieues* (high-rise suburbs), and singer-songwriters *à la* Jacques Brel. For traditional folk music at many summer festivals, see p28.

Theatre and Film

Well-subsidised local theatres feature adventurous programmes of music, dance, cabaret, stand-up comedy and plays. Some cinemas show English-language releases in *V.O.* or *version originale*, but dubbing (*V.F.* or *version française*) is the norm. France's thriving film industry turns out consistently well-made 'insider' glimpses of Gallic society.

Museums

Almost every large town has museums of local history; fine, contemporary and decorative art (*Beaux-Arts, L'Art Contemporain, Les Arts Décoratifs*); natural history etc. Some may be museum-pieces in themselves, others stylishly-designed and inventive. In rural areas, *Éco-musées* preserve local craft and farming traditions with workshops and demonstrations. State-run museums and galleries usually open on Sundays but close on Tuesdays and public holidays. Smaller museums or gardens may close for lunch and before dusk.

ports

ootball France's cup final is in May.
op league matches involving clubs
ch as 'PSG' (Paris-St-Germain,
onounced pay-ess-zhay) or
DM' (Olympique de Marseille,
onounced oh-wem) are a fine
ectacle.

aditional sports boat-jousting
a joute) at Lyon and Sète, see p29;
rsions of Royal tennis (*le jeu de
ume, la balle au tambourin; la pelote
sque*).

ullfighting Head south: especially
the Roman arenas of Nîmes and
les. By law, the bull is only killed
towns with more than a 50-year
story of corridas. *Rejoneadors*
orse-back fighters) and several
omen fighters are popular stars.
e Festivals, p28.

Where do you buy tickets?
On achète les billets, où?

eisure activities

egional tourist offices often
ganise group activity holidays –
ll for brochures. The *Institut
éographique National* publishes
cellent themed maps (golf courses,
mbing, hiking etc.

Megève, Haute Savoie

Municipal recreation grounds
(*bases de loisirs*) whose facilities include
watersports, golf, riding, picnicking,
tennis, climbing walls and play areas.
No membership; activities are often
free.

Les Country Clubs Private clubs
with restaurants, children's activities,
tennis courts, pools, often offering
daily/weekly membership, summer
tennis academies etc.

Bird-watching Camargue (flamin-
goes and Mediterranean waders;
spring/summer), Cap Sizun
(Brittany; nesting seabirds; spring/
early summer), Col d'Orgambidhexa
(Basque Pyrenees; migrating birds;
August–November).

Canoeing Popular on the gentle,
scenic Ardèche, Loire, Tarn and
Garonne rivers.

Cycling Mountain-biking (*le vélo tout-
terrain*) is a major craze. Ask at information offices or sports shops for
organised rides and bike hire.

Diving Good off many coastal
resorts. Try Finistère, Brittany and
the crystal-clear Calanques waters
near Marseille and Cassis.

Golf The compulsory insurance
licence (*assurance*) costs 20F per day.
Players may have to pass the green
card test demonstrating basic ability
(*carte verte*); beginners courses are
available.

Hunting, shooting and fishing

France teems with game, and hunting (*la chasse*) is widely practiced. Fishing tackle and gun shops can supply permits and information. Pyrenean rivers are famous for their trout. Some ports (Brittany, the south-east) operate regular sea-fishing trips .

Pétanque or boules

The 'national game', played throughout France on roadsides, beaches, car parks, squares and outdoor *boulodromes*. Players use elaborate techniques to pitch bowls at *le cochonnet* (the piglet), knocking their opponents' aside (nearest ball wins). Hang around, ask in French, and you may get a game or a drink at the clubhouse.

Riding

Accompanied treks staying at *gîtes d'étape* (see p46) are organised throughout rural France. Provence and the Camargue are popular destinations for trekking.

Swimming

Huge northern and Atlantic beaches have strong tides, surf, wet sand and shingle; they're seldom crowded outside the main resorts. Tideless Mediterranean beaches have soft sand and warm seas but can be narrow, dirty and crowded (go before 9.30 am or after 5 pm in summer; weekdays from May to early July, also September). Try the Camargue, or off-shore islands (Porquerolles) for more peace.

Surfing, sand-yachting, kayaking

Channel and Atlantic beaches.

Walking

classic long-distance walks (*chemins de grandes randonnées* or *GRs*) and local footpaths are all well marked. Paths in the south-east may be closed and patrolled in summer due to forest arson.

Windsurfing

Head south to the Camargue beaches of Piémanson and Fos, and the Landes (see pp20–23) or try inland lakes and reservoir.

Winter sports

Smaller, cheaper, enjoyable alternatives to the major resorts include Sauze and Super-Sauze (Alpes-de-Haute-Provence), Pas-de-la-Case and Andorra-la-Vella (Pyrenean principality of Andorra). Avoid French school holidays (Christmas, most of February, Easter). Monoskiing, snow-boarding and cross-country skiing are also popular.

> **!** I'd like to hire some skis.
> **Je voudrais louer des skis.**

Children

Note that, even in term-time, Wednesday is a holiday for younger children, so theme parks, McDonald etc are very busy. On the upside, children's activities flourish. Look out for children's theatre with *marionnettes*, mime and music; art workshops and tours feature at many museums. French kids love the technological attractions at the Futuroscope (Poitiers), and Parc de la Villette or the Palais de la Découverte (Paris). In summer, *Bas de Loisirs* and country clubs organise day courses (tennis, watersports, riding, archery) and many towns an resorts also provide day clubs (*les Centres Aérés*).

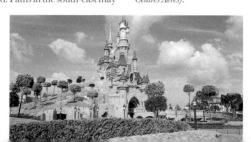

Phrasemaker
Getting to know the place

I'd like (a town plan/ an entertainment guide).	**Je voudrais (un plan de la ville/un guide des distractions).**
Do you have any information (in English)?	**Avez-vous des informations (en anglais)?**
What is there (to see/to do) here?	**Qu'est-ce qu'il y a (à voir/à faire) ici?**

Is there (a guided tour/ a bus tour)?	**Il y a (une visite guidée/un tour en bus)?**
Are there (any tennis courts/ any nightclubs) here?	**Il y a (des courts de tennis/des night-clubs) ici?**
Can you recommend me (a restaurant/a museum)?	**Vous pouvez me recommander (un restaurant/un musée)?**
What is there for children to do?	**Qu'est-ce qu'il y a pour les enfants?**

Voilà un guide.	Here's a guide (book or person).
Qu'est-ce qui vous intéresse?	What are you interested in?
Il y a un concert de (musique classique/jazz).	There is a (classical music/ jazz) concert.
Il y a des dégustations de vins.	There are wine-tasting sessions.

Rouen

93

Things to do or see

un ballet	ballet
le championnat de (boules/golf)	(bowls/golf) championship
un château	castle/mansion
un cirque	circus
(un club/le terrain) de golf	golf (club/course)
une course cycliste	cycle race
les courses automobiles	car racing
les courses de chevaux	horse racing
un défilé du Carnaval	carnival parade
une discothèque	disco
une école d'équitation	riding school
une exposition (de sculptures/de peintures)	(sculpture/painting) exhibition
un festival de (musique classique/jazz)	(classical music/jazz) festival
un feu d'artifice	fireworks
une galerie d'art	art gallery
une fête foraine	funfair
un match de (tennis/rugby/football)	(tennis/rugby/football) match
un musée	museum
un parc d'attractions	amusement park
une patinoire	ice rink
la pétanque	petanque (a form of bowls)
une piscine	swimming pool
les régates	regattas
un théâtre	theatre
un tournoi	tournament

Getting more information

See p40 for a list of places in town.

Where is (the swimming pool/ the beach/the concert hall)?	**Où est (la piscine/la plage/ la salle de concert)?**
Where does the tour start?	**Où commence le tour?**
At what time does it (start/ finish)?	**Ça (commence/finit) à quelle heure?**
When is it (open/closed)?	**Quand est-il (ouvert/fermé)?**
Do you need tickets?	**On a besoin de billets?**
Are there any tickets?	**Il y a des billets?**
Where do you buy tickets?	**On achète les billets où?**

Pas besoin de billets.	You don't need tickets.
Désolé/e, il ne reste plus de billets.	Sorry, it's sold out.
Sur la place à dix heures.	In the main square at 10am.
De neuf heures trente du matin à sept heures du soir.	From 9.30am to 7pm.
Au guichet.	At the ticket office.
Ici, sur (la carte/le plan).	Here, on (the map/plan).

Getting in

Do you have any tickets for . . . ?	**Avez-vous des billets pour . . . ?**
How much is it?	**Ça fait combien?**
Are there any concessions?	**Il y a des réductions?**
Two tickets, please, for (Saturday/tomorrow).	**Deux billets, s'il vous plaît, pour (samedi/demain).**
How long does it last?	**Ça dure combien de temps?**
Is the film subtitled?	**Le film est sous-titré?**
Is there a programme (in English)?	**Il y a un programme (en anglais)?**
Is there an interval?	**Il y a un entracte?**
Are the seats numbered?	**Les places sont numérotées?**
Is this seat (available/ taken)?	**Cette place est (libre/occupée)?**

Oui, moitié prix pour (étudiants/ enfants/retraités).	Yes, half price for (students/ children/pensioners).
Un entracte de vingt minutes.	One interval of 20 minutes.
Cette place est (libre/occupée).	This seat is (free/taken).
VO/version originale	foreign film in its original language
VF/version française	dubbed foreign film

Signs

balcon	circle
bar	bar
escalier	stairs
loge	box
orchestre	stalls
sortie	exit
toilettes dames/femmes	ladies' toilets
toilettes messieurs/hommes	men's toilets
vestiaires	cloakroom

Swimming and sunbathing

Can I use the hotel pool?	**Je peux utiliser la piscine de l'hôtel?**
Where are (the changing rooms/the showers)?	**Où sont (les vestiaires/les douches)?**
I'd like to hire a parasol.	**Je voudrais louer un parasol.**
air-bed	**un matelas pneumatique**
armbands	**des flotteurs**
bucket and spade	**un seau et une pelle**
deckchair	**une chaise longue**
life jacket	**un gilet (de sauvetage)**
mask and flippers	**un masque et des palmes**
rubber ring	**une bouée**
towel	**une serviette**
sand castle	**un château de sable**
suntan lotion	**de la crème solaire**
sunglasses	**des lunettes de soleil**
(indoor/outdoors) swimming pool	**une piscine (couverte/en plein air)**
swimsuit/trunks	**un maillot (de bain)**
windbreak	**un coupe-vent**

Signs

caution	deposit
courant violent	strong current
location	hiring/hire
marée (basse/haute)	(low/high) tide
premiers secours	first aid
profond/profondeur	deep/depth

Sports

Where can I go (swimming/snorkelling)?	**Où puis-je (nager/nager avec un tuba)?**
Where can I go (fishing/bungee jumping)?	**Où puis-je (aller à la pêche/sauter à l'élastique)?**
Where can I play (golf)?	**Où puis-je jouer (au golf)?**

Where can I go (hiking/ cross-country skiing)?	**Où puis-je faire (une randonnée pédestre/du ski de fond)?**
I'd like to hire (a racket/skates/ a boat).	**Je voudrais louer (une raquette/ des patins/un bateau).**
I'd like to take (sailing/ skiing lessons).	**Je voudrais prendre des cours (de voile/de ski).**
How much is it (per hour/ per day)?	**C'est combien (de l'heure/par jour)?**
downhill skiing	**le ski de descente**
horse riding	**l'équitation (f)**

ice-skating	**le patinage sur glace**	sailing	**la voile**
pony trekking	**une randonnée équestre**	scuba diving	**la plongée sous-marine**
pot-holing	**la spéléo- logie**	skiing	**le ski**
rock-climbing	**la varappe**	surfing	**le surf**
roller skating/ rollerblading	**le patin (à roulettes/ en ligne)**	tennis	**le tennis**
		table tennis	**le ping-pong**
		tobogganing	**la luge**
		water-skiing	**du ski nautique**
rowing	**l'aviron (m)**	windsurfing	**la planche à voile**

Sports equipment

I'd like (to hire) a . . .	**Je voudrais (louer) . . .**	sailing boat	**un bateau à voiles**
ball (rugby ball/football)	**un ballon (de rugby/ de foot)**	sailing dinghy	**un dériveur**
rubber dinghy	**un canot pneumatique**	surfboard/ windsurfing board	**une planche (de surf/ à voile)**
motor boat	**un bateau à moteur**	tennis (racket/ ball)	**(une raquette/ balle) de tennis**
oars	**des rames**		
rowing boat	**un bateau à rames**		

Skiing

cable car	**le téléphérique**	skis	**des skis**
ski boots	**des chaussures de ski**	toboggan	**une luge**
ski pass	**un forfait de ski**		
ski run/track	**la piste**		
ski suit	**une combinaison de ski**		
ski tow	**le tire-fesses**		
ski lift	**le télésiège**		

Dieppe

97

Sound Check

g is pronounced in three ways, depending on the letter which follows it

g + a, o, u or **consonant (except n)** – like 'g' in 'ground'

guide	geed
golf	golf
programme	prohgram

g + n – like 'ni' in 'onion'

champagne	shompahnye
Dordogne	doardonye

g + e or **i** – like 's' in 'measure'

gilet	jeelay
patinage	patinaj

Practise on these words: **guichet, plongée, guidée, baignoire**

Language works

Getting to know the place

1 Finding out about local activities

- **Bonjour, Madame, je voudrais un plan de la ville, s'il vous plaît.**
- □ **Voilà. Qu'est-ce qui vous intéresse?**
- **Qu'est-ce qu'il y a à faire et à voir dans la région?**
- □ **Il y a des randonnées équestres et pédestres, un championnat de boules, des musées.**
- **Il y a des expositions de peintures?**
- □ **Oui, au musée d'art.**

What is there to see and do?

Getting more information

2 Finding out about a tour of an art gallery

- **Bonjour, Monsieur. La visite guidée commence à quelle heure, s'il vous plaît?**
- □ **À neuf heures.**
- **On achète les billets où?**
- □ **Pas besoin de billets!**
- **Ah bon! Où commence la visite?**
- □ **Ici, Madame.**

A ticket is/isn't necessary.

Getting in

3 At the museum

- **Bonsoir, vous désirez?**
- □ **Deux billets pour le musée, s'il vous plaît. Il y a des réductions pour les enfants?**
- **Oui, moitié prix.**
- □ **Bon, un adulte et un enfant s'il vous plaît.**

Children pay full/half price.

Swimming

4 At a pool

- **Excusez-moi, Mademoiselle, où sont les vestiaires?**
- □ **À droite, en face des douches.**
- **Je voudrais louer deux serviettes, s'il vous plaît. C'est combien?**
- □ **Dix francs et il y a une caution de cinquante francs.**
- **Ah bon. Voilà.**

Total cost . . .

Sports

5 Enquiring about water-skiing lessons

- ■ **Je voudrais prendre des cours de ski nautique.**
- □ **Bien sûr, Monsieur!**
- ■ **C'est combien?**
- □ **C'est cent cinquante francs la demi-heure.**
- ■ **Une heure, s'il vous plaît.**

A lesson costs . . . for . . .

Try it out

Matching pairs

Complete the sentence by matching the objects with the places

Je peux voir . . .
1 **des patins**
2 **des billets**
3 **des châteaux de sable**
4 **des télésièges**

a **sur la piste de ski**
b **à la plage**
c **au guichet**
d **à la patinoire**

Excuse me . . .

How would you say the following in French?
1 What time does it finish?
2 Do I need tickets?
3 What is there for children to do?
4 Is that seat available?
5 How long does the performance last?
6 How much is a lesson per hour?

As if you were there

Asking for a guidebook at a museum

- ■ **Bonjour, vous désirez?**
- □ (Say hello and ask for a guide book to the museum, in English)
- ■ **Mais oui! Voilà un guide en anglais.**
- □ (Say thanks and ask how much the guide book is)
- ■ **Quinze francs cinquante, s'il vous plaît.**

Emergencies

Crime

France is on a par with most Western countries – muggings occur and conspicuous tourists may be targets. Some places (ie Marseille) have mad, bad reputations; wherever you are, keep valuables out of sight in a closed bag; leave nothing in your car, even stereos. Women should, as anywhere, avoid walking alone at night. Racial attacks are, sadly, not uncommon. Hawkers gather at tourist sights (never aggressive, but watch your pockets). Approved street vendors sell magazines helping the homeless. Look out for *L'Itinérant* or *Macadam*.

Help!
Au secours!

Dealing with the police

If you are robbed, it is sensible not to resist. Report all incidents immediately to the local police, who will provide an insurance report.

French police are armed, with extensive stop-and-search powers and may detain anyone for 48 hours (the so-called *garde à vue*), with no right to an outside call. If you are stopped, remain calm and cooperative.

Health tips

Pharmacies (neon green cross signs) can recommend treatments or doctors (*un médecin généraliste*). After hours, and on Sundays or holidays, call directory enquiries for *SOS Médecins* (home visits, usually within the hour); the local police station (*le commissariat*) will direct you to the duty pharmacy (show your prescription, *ordonnance*), and will telephone ahead with your name. Visits must be paid in cash or Eurocheques. For insurance claims, ask for and keep, the brown form (*la feuille de soins*) given by the doctor. EU nationals should show a stamped E111 form (available from post offices before departure). No special vaccinations are needed for France.

I'd like something for sunburn, please.
Je voudrais quelque chose pour les coups de soleil, s'il vous plaît.

Drinking water is always marked *eau potable*. Other taps are, by law, labelled *eau non-potable*. Domestic tap water is usually OK, but buy *eau minérale* if in doubt.
Mosquitoes are a nocturnal nuisance everywhere from April to October. A plug-in diffuser (*un diffuseur*) zaps them even with open windows (available with refills at all super-markets). Use repellent out of doors at night.
Vipers and boar are common in all forests; scorpions are found in the south-west and Montpellier area, and wolves in the southern Alps. All are very shy; ticks are a less bashful summer predator in dense woodland.
Take precautions against sunburn especially in the south. The hottest part of the day is 2 pm in summer.
Meat is cooked pink, and sauces (eg *hollandaise* or *mayonnaise*) may contain lightly-cooked or raw egg. Pregnant women should avoid these and the many unpasteurised cheeses (*au lait cru*).

Standards of toilets vary – smelly shower-pan toilets still lurk at the back of many cafés and restaurants. Ask for *les WC* (pronounced 'vay-say') or *toilettes*; 'H' for men (*hommes*), 'F' for women (*femmes*). Attendants should be given a small tip. Bars usually allow passers-by to use their toilets.

Telephones

You'll need to invest in a *Télécarte* (50 or 120 units) from any *tabac*. You won't find many coin-operated machines in France. Some phones take foreign credit cards (Visa or Mastercard/Eurocard) with your PIN number. France has 10-digit numbers including a regional code (eg 01 for Paris). For international calls, dial 00 and your country code (listed in phone booths). To call collect, dial 00 33 and your country code for free access to an operator back home.

Post offices

La Poste is always clearly signposted, and decked in bright yellow-and-blue livery. Opening times vary. Yellow machines relieve the queues in larger offices: weigh your mail, insert the cash required and take a printed label in place of a stamp. Larger post offices have fax machines (*Publifax*). You can also buy stamps at *tabacs*.

I want to send this to Australia, please.
Je voudrais envoyer ça en Australie, s'il vous plaît.

Breakdown and recovery

Motorways have numbered emergency telephones every mile and a

bit; motorway police (*la gendarmerie*) will locate your call and arrange towing etc.

On other roads, call directory enquiries from the nearest phone for the numbers of local services (*dépannages* et *remorquages d'automobiles*). You'll need to pay on the spot (Visa and possibly Mastercard or Eurocard). Contact your hirer or insurer.

Special needs travellers

Disabled parking spaces are strictly enforced in all car parks. Public transport is less accessible (but see p38 for the TGV). The Louvre has possibly the world's grandest wheel-chair entrance – an open lift down into the famous pyramid. Travellers needing help at Paris Charles-de-Gaulle/Roissy and Orly airports can call 01 46 75 15 65 (in advance). Check car hire options with the main international hirers before leaving.

Useful telephone numbers

Ambulance (*SAMU*): 15
Police: 17
Fire brigade (*les pompiers*): 18
Directory enquiries: 12
International directory enquiries: 12
Embassies (all in Paris)
Australian: 4 rue Jean Rey, 15th arr. 01 40 59 33 00
British: 35 rue Faubourg-St-Honoré, 8th arr. 01 44 51 31 00
Canadian: 35 av. Montaigne, 8th arr. 01 44 43 29 00
Irish: 12 av. Foch, 16th arr. 01 44 17 67 00
New Zealand: 7 ter, rue Léonard-de-Vinci, 16th arr. 01 45 00 24 11
South African: 59 quai d'Orsay, 7th arr. 01 45 55 92 37
US: 2 av. Gabriel, 8th arr. 01 43 12 22 92

Phrasemaker
General

Help!	**Au secours!**
Hello there!	**Hé!**
Can you help me?	**Pouvez-vous m'aider?**
Where's (the police station/ the hospital)?	**Où est (le poste de police/ l'hôpital)?**
Where's the nearest (petrol station/garage/chemist)?	**Où est (la station service/le garage/la pharmacie) le/la plus proche?**
Thank you.	**Merci.**
Leave me alone.	**Laissez-moi tranquille.**
I'll call the police.	**Je vais appeler la police.**

Health

(A doctor/An ambulance) is needed.	**Il faut (un docteur/une ambulance).**
It's urgent.	**C'est urgent.**
Does anyone speak English?	**Quelqu'un parle anglais?**
Don't move (me/him)!	**Ne (me/le) bougez pas!**
I'd like an appointment with (a doctor/a dentist).	**Je voudrais un rendez-vous avec (un docteur/un dentiste).**

Parts of the body

ankle	**la cheville**	knee	**le genou**
arm	**le bras**	leg	**la jambe**
back	**le dos**	liver	**le foie**
chest/bust	**la poitrine**	mouth	**la bouche**
ear	**une oreille**	neck	**le cou**
ear drum	**le tympan**	nose	**le nez**
eye	**un œil**	shoulders	**les épaules**
eyes	**les yeux**	stomach	**l'estomac**
foot	**le pied**	teeth	**les dents**
hand	**la main**	throat	**la gorge**
head	**la tête**	tooth	**la dent**
hips	**les hanches**	tummy	**le ventre**
kidneys	**les reins**	wrist	**le poignet**

Common symptoms

I've got (diarrhoea/indigestion).	**J'ai (la diarrhée/une indigestion).**
I'm constipated.	**Je suis constipé/e.**
I've got a (cold/cough).	**J'ai un rhume/Je tousse.**
I've got (a rash/shivers).	**J'ai des rougeurs/des frissons.**
flu	**J'ai la grippe.**
(I've/He's been) sick (all night).	**(J'ai/Il a) vomi (toute la nuit).**
It hurts (here).	**Ça fait mal (ici).**
I've got (back ache/sore eyes).	**J'ai mal (au dos/aux yeux).**
I've got (stomach-ache/earache).	**J'ai mal (à l'estomac/à l'oreille).**

Common accidents and conditions

I've (cut/burnt) myself.	**Je me suis (coupé/brûlé).**
I've been (bitten/stung).	**J'ai été (mordu/piqué).**
I can't (move/feel) my leg.	**Je ne peux pas (bouger/sentir) ma jambe.**
I'm allergic to (antibiotics/animals).	**Je suis allergique aux (antibiotiques/animaux).**
I'm (diabetic/pregnant/epileptic).	**Je suis (diabétique/enceinte/épileptique).**
I have asthma.	**J'ai de l'asthme.**
I wear contact lenses.	**Je porte des lentilles de contact.**
My child has a temperature.	**Mon enfant a de la température.**
(She/He) feels (sick/dizzy).	**(Elle/Il) a (la nausée/le vertige).**
Can I have a treatment sheet?	**Je voudrais une feuille de soins.**
I have (toothache/a broken tooth).	**J'ai (mal aux dents/une dent cassée).**
I've lost (a filling/a crown).	**J'ai perdu (un plombage/une couronne).**

(C'est/Ce n'est pas) grave.	(It's/It isn't) serious.
C'est (une entorse/une fracture/un claquage).	It's (a sprain/a fracture/a pulled muscle).
Il faut (faire une opération/aller à l'hôpital).	You need (an operation/to go to the hospital).
Voilà une ordonnance.	Here's a prescription.
Je vous mets un plombage (provisoire).	I'll put a (temporary) filling in.
Il faut arracher la dent.	I'll have to take the tooth out.

103

At the chemist's

I'd like something for . . .	**Je voudrais quelque chose . . .**
a hangover	**pour la gueule de bois**
period pains	**pour les douleurs de règles**
(air/sea) sickness	**contre le mal (de l'air/de mer)**
a sore throat	**pour le mal de gorge**
insect stings	**pour les piqûres d'insectes**
sunburn.	**contre les coups de soleil.**
Do you have any . . .	**Avez-vous . . .**
after-sun lotion	**une lotion après-soleil**
aspirin	**de l'aspirine**
condoms	**des préservatifs**
cough mixture	**du sirop**
painkillers	**un analgésique**
plasters?	**des pansements adhésifs?**

Qu'est-ce que vous avez mangé/bu?	What have you eaten/drunk?
Vous prenez déjà des médicaments?	Are you already taking any other medicine?
C'est pour (vous/ un enfant)?	Is it for (you/a child)?
Un paquet de six?	A packet of six?

URGENCES | EMERGENCY

Advice

Prenez/Appliquez . . .	Take/Apply . . .
ces cachets/comprimés	these tablets
cette lotion/ce médicament	this lotion /this medicine
ces pilules	these pills
cette pommade/des supposi-toires/du sirop	this ointment/some supposi-tories/some cough mixture
(avant/après) les repas	(before/after) meals
avec de l'eau/à jeun	with water/on an empty stomach
une cuillerée (une/deux) fois par jour.	one spoonful (one/two) times a day.
Ne pas prendre plus de trois fois (par jour/en 24h).	Do not take more than three times (a day/in 24hrs).
Risque de somnolence.	May cause drowsiness.
Avaler sans croquer.	Swallow whole.
Mâcher, ne pas avaler entier.	Chew, do not swallow whole.
Ne pas utiliser près des yeux.	Avoid eye contact.
Il faut (rester au lit/vous reposer/boire beaucoup d'eau).	You must (stay in bed/rest/drink lots of water).
Il ne faut pas (vous lever/courir/faire des efforts).	You mustn't (get up/run/take exercise).
C'est (une intoxication alimentaire/une crise de foie).	It's (food poisoning/overeating rich food).

Words to listen out for

l'abcès	abcess	**infection**	infection
l'appendicite	appendicitis	**insolation**	sunstroke
bronchite	bronchitis	**l'omoplate**	shoulder blade
cassé	broken	**les oreillons**	mumps
clavicule	collarbone	**l'os**	bone
cœur	heart	**otite**	ear infection
colonne vertébrale	spine	**pneumonie**	pneumonia
		poumons	lungs
commotion cérébrale	concussion	**rougeole**	measles
		sinusite	sinus infection
contagieux	contagious	**ulcère**	stomach ulcer
côte	rib	**varicelle**	chickenpox

Car breakdown

I've broken down . . .	**Je suis en panne . . .**
on the motorway (A10)	**sur l'autoroute (A10)**
(ten) kilometres from . . .	**à (dix) kilomètres de . . .**
(The engine/The steering) isn't working.	**(Le moteur/La direction) ne marche pas.**
The brakes aren't working.	**Les freins ne marchent pas.**
It won't start.	**Elle ne démarre pas.**
I've got a flat tyre.	**J'ai un pneu crevé.**
The battery's flat.	**La batterie est à plat.**
I've run out of petrol.	**J'ai une panne d'essence.**
When will it be ready?	**Ça sera prêt quand?**

Car parts

l'accélérateur	accelerator	**les feux**	lights
la batterie	battery	**les freins**	brakes
la boite de vitesse	gearbox	**le pare-brise**	windscreen
		le pare-choc	bumper
la bougie	spark plug	**la pédale**	pedal
le capot	bonnet	**les phares**	headlights
les codes	dipped lights	**le pneu**	tyre
la courroie de ventilateur	fan belt	**la portière**	car door
		le radiateur	radiator
le cric	jack	**la roue**	wheel
l'embrayage	clutch	**le tuyau d'échappement**	exhaust pipe
les essuie-glace	wipers		
		le volant	steering wheel

Theft or loss

I've lost (my wallet/ my passport/ my son/ my daughter).	**J'ai perdu (mon portefeuille/ mon passeport/ mon fils/ ma fille).**
I've had (my watch/ my bag) stolen.	**On m'a volé (ma montre/ mon sac).**
I've been (attacked/ mugged).	**J'ai été (attaqué/ agressé).**
My car has been broken into.	**On a forcé la porte de ma voiture.**
Yesterday (morning/evening /afternoon).	**Hier (matin/soir/ après-midi).**
This morning.	**Ce matin.**
In (a store/a cafe).	**Dans (un magasin/ un café).**

Valuables

my bracelet	**mon bracelet**	my necklace	**mon collier**
my briefcase	**ma serviette**	my passport	**mon passeport**
my camcorder	**mon camé-scope**	my purse	**mon porte-monnaie**
my camera	**mon appareil-photo**	my ring	**ma bague**
my car	**ma voiture**	my rucksack	**mon sac à dos**
my coat	**mon manteau**	my suitcase	**ma valise**
my driving licence	**mon permis (de conduire)**	some tickets	**des billets**
my handbag	**mon sac à main**	my traveller's cheques	**mes travellers**
my jewellery	**mes bijoux**	my wallet	**mon porte-feuille**
some money	**de l'argent**		

Quelle couleur?	What colour is it?
Quelle heure?	What time?
Qu'est-ce qu'il y a dedans?	What's in it?
Où (l'avez-vous perdu)?	Where (did you lose it)?
Quand (avez-vous réalisé)?	When (did you realize)?
Quel est . . .	What's . . .
votre nom et votre adresse?	your name and address?
votre numéro de passeport?	your passport number?
le numéro d'immatriculation	your car's registration number?
la marque de voiture?	your car's make?
Remplissez cette fiche.	Fill in this form.
Revenez plus tard.	Come back later.

Language works

Doctors and chemists

1 Explaining symptoms
- ■ **Bonjour, docteur; j'ai vomi toute la nuit, j'ai mal à l'estomac.**
- □ **Ça fait mal ici?**
- ■ **Oui! Et j'ai mal à la tête.**
- □ **Qu'est-ce que vous avez mangé?**
- ■ **Fruits de mer, poulet, gâteau à la crème.**
- □ **Mmm . . . c'est une intoxication alimentaire. Il faut rester au lit et boire beaucoup d'eau.**

The doctor asked what the patient ate/drank.
The patient should stay in bed and . . .

2 Asking for medicine at the chemist's
- ■ **Je voudrais quelque chose contre la diarrhée.**
- □ **C'est pour vous?**
- ■ **Oui.**
- □ **Bon, voilà des cachets. Il faut boire beaucoup d'eau.**
- ■ **Oui! Je voudrais quelque chose contre le mal de mer pour un enfant.**
- □ **Voilà des comprimés. Ne pas prendre plus d'une fois par jour!**

Take the sea sickness tablets once/no more than once a day.

Theft or loss

3 Reporting a lost handbag
- ■ **J'ai perdu mon sac. Il est en cuir.**
- □ **Quelle couleur?**
- ■ **Marron et noir.**
- □ **Qu'est-ce qu'il y a dedans?**
- ■ **Il y a des travellers, de l'argent.**
- □ **Remplissez cette fiche, s'il vous plaît.**

(en cuir = leather)

The clerk filled/didn't fill in the form.

Try it out

Take your medicine

Read the labels below and work out what you should and shouldn't do.
1 **Deux cuillerées trois fois par jour avant les repas.**
2 **Prenez aux repas.**
3 **Ne pas prendre plus de trois fois par jour.**
4 **Ne pas utiliser près des yeux.**
5 **Prenez à jeun.**

As if you were there

At the chemist's you ask for some painkillers
- ■ **Bonjour, je peux vous aider?**
- □ (Say you've got a headache. Ask for some painkillers)
- ■ **Vous êtes allergique à l'aspirine?**
- □ (Say no)
- ■ **Voilà de l'Aspro®. Un paquet de six ou un paquet de douze?**
- □ (Say a packet of twelve, please. Ask how much it is)

Sound Check

Take care to distinguish between the following vowel sounds **eu**, **œu** and **ou** or **oue**

yeux	yur
cœur	cur
genou	jenou
toux	tou

but

ouest	ouest

Practise on these words: **bouche, coupé, beurre**

Language builder

Gender

All French nouns (words for things, people or animals) are either feminine or masculine. A noun's gender affects:
– the form of 'a', 'the' and 'of' used before it
– most adjectives used after it.

Most nouns ending in **-age**, **-ment** or **-oir** are masculine.

Most nouns ending in **-ance**, **-ence**, **-té** and **-ion** are feminine.

People's gender is obvious, **le garçon**, **une dame**, but it doesn't really matter if you can't remember the gender of other nouns as you'll still be understood!

'a' and 'the': the articles

'a'
Feminine: **une**
une voiture   (a car)

Masculine: **un**
un journal   (a newspaper)

'the':
Feminine: **la**
la pomme   (the apple)

Masculine: **le**
le magasin   (the shop)

before a vowel: **l'**
l' église   (the church)
l' hôpital   (the hospital)

Plural
Feminine and masculine: **les**
les chaussures   (the shoes)

Nouns in the plural change their endings. Usually, this just means a silent 's' is added.
une voiture   deux voitures

Some, any, of and from

In French you use the same word, **de**. This is how **de** changes:

Feminine nouns
de + la: *de la*
de la confiture   (some jam)

before a vowel and 'h'
de + l':
de l' eau   (some water)
de l' hôtel   (of the hotel)

Masculine
de + le: *du*
du magasin   (of the shop)

Plural
Feminine and masculine
de + les: *des*
des chaussures   (some shoes)

some:
Je voudrais de la limonade
I would like some lemonade

any:
Avez-vous des pommes?
Have you got any apples?

of:
une bouteille de vin
a bottle of wine

of the:
une carte de la région
a map of the region

from:
Je viens de Londres
I come from London

Quantity

De is also used as part of some words of quantity. Here it doesn't change at all.

a lot of/much/many:
beaucoup de vin
a lot of/much wine

a little (a small quantity):
un peu de vin
a little wine

more/less:
plus de/moins de fromage
more/less cheese

how much/how many:
combien de jours?
how many days?

Questions

Simple questions
There are three ways to ask a simple question in French.

1 Use the same form as for the statement, but raise your intonation on the last word:
Vous voulez une orange.
You want an orange.
Vous voulez une orange?
Do you want an orange?

2 Start with the phrase **est-ce que** and leave the rest of the sentence as it is:

la place des Vosges, Paris

Est-ce que vous voulez une orange?
Do you want an orange?

3 Turn the verb (action word) and the subject of the verb round:
Voulez-vous une orange?
Do you want an orange?

What? questions
If you want to ask a What? question, do one of the following:
1 Start with **que** and follow it with the verb and the subject of the verb turned around:
Que voulez-vous?
What do you want?

2 Start with the phrase **qu'est-ce que** and leave the rest of the sentence as it is:
Qu'est-ce que vous voulez?
What do you want?

What is/what are? questions
If you want to ask a What is/what are? question or ask about a noun use **quel** or **quelle**. Use **quels** or **quelles** when the noun is plural.
Quel est le prix?
What is the price?
Quels sandwichs avez-vous?
What kind of sandwiches have you got?

Negatives

To make a sentence negative in French you wrap **ne . . . pas** round the verb. You'll often hear the French drop the **ne** and you'll be understood if you do too!

Je ne suis pas Français.
I am not French.
Ça ne va pas!
It's not all right!/I'm not well.
Je ne comprends pas.
I don't understand.

before a vowel **ne**: **n'**
Je n'ai pas de monnaie.
I don't have any change.

Others

There are other negative terms which you can use in the same way:

Il n'en reste plus.
There is no more (left).

Je ne roule jamais vite.
I never drive fast.

Je ne vois rien.
I see nothing/don't see anything.

Il n'y a personne.
There is nobody.

Il n'y a ni bus ni train.
There are neither buses nor trains.

Je n'ai que dix francs. or
j'ai seulement dix francs.
I only have ten francs.

Je n'ai pas de monnaie.
I don't have any change.

Adjectives

Adjective describe nouns and change according to the gender. If they don't already end in 'e',

they add an 'e' if the noun is feminine. In plural they add 's'. The 's' is usually silent, but the 'e' often makes the last consonant hard.

French adjectives usually come after the noun, with the following exceptions:
all numbers and cardinal numbers (first **premier**, second **deuxième**, third **troisième**);

small	petit	petite
tall/large	grand	grande
young	jeune	jeune
old	vieux	vieille
	vieil	
pretty	joli	jolie
beautiful	beau/bel	belle
good	bon	bonne
bad	mauvais	mauvaise
big	gros	grosse
excellent	excellent	excellente
short	court	courte
kind	gentil	gentille
new	nouveau	nouvelle
a red car	une auto rouge	
a ripe melon	un melon mûr	

Possessions

Use **de** to show possession:
le passeport de la dame
the lady's passport

To talk about 'my car', 'his watch', etc, French uses the following forms. These change according to the gender of the item possessed, not the gender of the owner.

Singular		
my	**mon**	**ma**
your	**ton**	**ta**
his/her	**son**	**sa**
our	**notre**	**notre**
your	**votre**	**votre**
their	**leur**	**leur**

Plural
for both masculine and feminine nouns

my	**mes**
your	**tes**
his/her	**ses**
our	**nos**
your	**vos**
their	**leur/s**

This, that, these, those

These words behave like adjectives, agreeing with the noun in gender and in number (singular or plural).

Masculine
ce melon	this melon
ces melons	these melons

Feminine
cette table	this table
ces tables	these tables

If you just want to point out an object it's much easier to use **ça**.

I want that!   **Je voudrais ça!**

Talking to people

In French there are two ways of saying 'you': an informal and a formal way. It's best to stick to the formal way **vous** unless talking to children when you should use **tu**, but don't worry if you can't remember.

Tu veux une glace?
Would you like an ice-cream?

Verbs

The endings of French verbs change according to who does the action and when. In French the Present tense means both 'I speak' and 'I am speaking'.

Regular verbs
Most infinitives (as found in a dictionary) end in '**er**', eg **parler**, to speak. Remove the last two letters and add the relevant ending:
je parle	**nous parlons**
tu parles	**vous parlez**
il/elle parle	**ils/elles parlent**

Irregular verbs
aller: to go
je vais	I go/I'm going
tu vas	you go
il/elle va	he/she goes
nous allons	we go/we're going
vous allez	you go
ils/elles vont	they go/they're going

avoir: to have
j'ai	I have
tu as	you have
il/elle a	he/she has
nous avons	we have
vous avez	you have
ils/elles ont	they have

être: to be
je suis	I am
tu es	you are
il/elle est	he/she is
nous sommes	we are
vous êtes	you are
ils/elles sont	they are

faire: to make/do
je fais	I do
tu fais	you do
il/elle fait	he/she does
nous faisons	we do
vous faites	you do
ils/elles font	they do

Answers

Bare necessities

1 8 Fr, 39; £40 is worth 305 Fr, 6.
2 24 Fr, 75.

As if you were there
- □ Bonjour (Monsieur), ça va. Et vous?
- □ Je suis de (your town). Je m'appelle (your name). Je vous présente (ma femme/mon mari. . .).
- □ Oui, merci beaucoup.

Crossed lines
1 b; 2 d; 3 a; 4 c

Getting around

1 After the traffic lights.
2 The driver's licence.
3 The toll.
4 It leaves at 14.28; it isn't direct.
5 Platform eight; don't forget to validate the tickets!

What's missing?
1 tout droit
2 passez le pont
3 faites le plein
4 je voudrais louer une voiture.

As if you were there
- ■ Pardon Monsieur, il y a une station d'essence près d'ici?
- ■ Merci, et pour aller sur l'autoroute?
- ■ Il y a un péage?

Somewhere to stay

1 200 Fr; breakfast isn't included.
2 Breakfast is from 6.30am.
3 It's 104 Fr altogether.
4 4000 Fr a week; rent doesn't include electricity – there's a meter.

Mix and match
1 c; 2 d; 3 e; 4 b; 5 a

What's missing?
1 complet; 2 cher; 3 combien
4 chambre

As if you were there
- ■ Bonjour, je voudrais une chambre.
- ■ Pour deux adultes.
- ■ La chambre à grand lit, s'il vous plaît.
- ■ Pour trois nuits. C'est combien par nuit? Le petit déjeuner est compris?

Buying things

1 140 Fr a kilo.
2 Strawberries.
3 They did have blue trousers left.
4 On the second floor.
5 One stamp costs 4 Fr.
6 Yes, in three hours time.

Match up
1 b; 2c; 3d; 4a

As if you were there
- □ Bonjour, je voudrais ça; qu'est-ce que c'est?
- □ Bon! J'en voudrais une autre, s'il vous plaît. C'est combien?

Café life

1 He suggests white, red or rosé wine.

As if you were there
- □ Je voudrais un citron pressé, sans glaçons, un thé au lait et un verre de vin blanc.
- □ Quels sandwichs avez-vous?
- □ Je voudrais un américain et une glace au chocolat.

Odd one out

1 un jus de raisin (a drink)
2 une glace au chocolat (an ice-cream)

Eating out

1 The house wine.
2 She suggests couscous aux légumes.

Jumbled up menu

1	a	4	d
2	f	5	c
3	b	6	e

As if you were there

□ Je voudrais les artichauts, comme hors-d'œuvre, et les moules, comme plat principal. C'est garni?
□ Une salade (verte) comme accompagnement, s'il vous plaît.
□ Un verre de vin blanc (s'il vous plaît).

Entertainment and leisure

1 Hiking and pony trekking, a bowls competition, museums, a painting exhibition.
2 A ticket isn't necessary.
3 Children pay half price.
4 10 Fr + 50 Fr deposit.
5 300 Fr an hour.

Matching pairs
1 d; 2 c; 3 b; 4 a

Excuse me . . .

1 Ça finit à quelle heure ?
2 On a besoin de billets?
3 Qu'est-ce qu'il y a pour les enfants?
4 Cette place est libre?
5 Ça dure combien de temps?
6 C'est combien de l'heure?

As if you were there

□ Bonjour, je voudrais un guide du musée en anglais.
□ Merci. Ça fait combien, le guide?/ Le guide, ça fait combien?

Emergencies

1 What the patient ate; drink lots of water.
2 No more than once a day.
3 The clerk didn't fill in the form, he asked you to do it.

Take your medicine
1 Take two spoonfuls, three times a day, before meals.
2 Take with food.
3 Don't take more than three times a day.
4 Don't use near eyes.
5 Take on an empty stomach.

As if you were there

□ J'ai mal à la tête. Avez-vous un analgésique?
□ Non.
□ Un paquet de douze, s'il vous plaît. Ça fait combien?

Dictionary

(see also Menu reader, p80)

à at/to
à demain see you tomorrow
à partir de from
abcès, l' (m) abcess
accélérateur, l' (m) accelerator
accompagnement, l' (m) side dish
acheter to buy
adhésif/sive sticky
adresse, l' (f) address
adulte, l' (m) adult
aération, l' (f) ventilation
aéroport, l' (m) airport
agence, l' (f) agency
aider to help
aimable helpful/kind
air, l' (m) air
ajouter to add
alcoolisé/e alcoholic
alimentation, l' (f) food store
aller to go
aller-retour, l' (m) return ticket
aller-simple, l' (m) single ticket
allergique allergic
allongé/e diluted/lying down
allumette, l' (f) match/thinly cut chips
alors so/then
ambulance, l' (f) ambulance
américain/e American/ham salad sandwich
ampoule, l' (f) blister/light bulb
analgésique, l' (m) pain killer
animal, l' (m) animal
antibiotique, l' (m) antibiotics
apéritif, l' (m) aperitif
appareil-photo, l' (m) camera
appartement, l' (m) appartment
appel, l' (m) call
appeler to call
appendicite, l' (f) appendicitis
appétit, l' (m) appetite
appliquer to apply
apporter to bring
après after
après-midi, l' (m/f) afternoon

argent, l' (m) money/silver
arracher to extract/pull out
arrêt, l' (m) stop
art, l' (m) art
artifice, le feu d' fireworks
ascenseur, l (m) lift
aspirine, l' (f) aspirin
assez enough/fairly
assiette, l' (f) plate
assurance, l' (f) insurance
asthme, l' (m) asthma
attendre to wait for
attention! watch out!/be careful
attraction, l' (f) amusement
au at/to the
au secours! Help!
auberge, l' (f) inn
aujourd'hui today
autoroute, l' (f) motorway
autre other
avaler to swallow
avant before
avant-hier the day before yesterday
avec with
avion, l' (m) aeroplane
aviron, l' (m) rowing
avocat, l' (m) avocado/lawyer
avoir (p111) to have
avoir besoin de to need
avoir mal to have a pain

bague, la ring
baguette, la long French stick
baignoire, la bathtub
bain, le bath
balade, la stroll
balcon, le balcony/circle (theatre)
balle, la small ball/bullet
ballet, le ballet
ballon, le large ball/balloon
banc, le bench
banque, la bank
bar, le bar
bas/se low
bateau, le boat
batterie, la battery (car)/drums (music)
beau/belle beautiful
beaucoup much/many/a lot

beauté, la beauty
bidet, le bidet
bien well
bien sûr of course
bijou, le jewel
bijouterie, la jeweller's
bikini, le bikini
billet, le ticket/banknote
biscuit, le biscuit
blanc/he white
bleu/e blue
blond/e blond
boire to drink
bois, le wood
boisson, la drink
boîte, la box/tin/can/night club
boîte de vitesses, la gear box
bon/ne good
bonbon, le sweet
bonjour hello (all day)
bonsoir good evening
bouche, la mouth
boucherie, la butcher's shop
bouchon, le cork
boucle d'oreille, la earring
bouée, la buoy/rubber ring
bouger to move
bougie, la candle/spark plug
boulangerie, la bakery
bouteille, la bottle
bracelet, le bracelet
bras, le arm
brillant/e shiny/glossy
broche, la brooch
bronchite, la bronchitis
brûlé/e burnt
brûlure, la burn
brun/e brown
bureau de tabac, le tobacconist
bus, le autobus

c'est it is/is it
ça that/it
ça va it's OK/I am/you are OK
cacao, le cocoa
cachet, le tablet
cadeau, le gift
caisse, la cash till
calissons, les (mpl) almond sweets
caméscope, le, camcorder (trade mark)

campagne, la countryside
camper to camp
camping, le campsite/camping
camping-car, le caravanette
canot, le dinghy
car, le coach/bus
carafe, la carafe
caramel, le soft toffee
caravane, la caravan
carnaval, le carnival
carrefour, le crossroad
carte, la map/card/menu
carte postale, la post card
carton, le carton/cardbord
cassé/e broken
caution, la deposit
ce (m) this
cédez (le passage) give way
ceinture, la belt
cendrier, le ashtray
centre commercial, le shopping centre
centre-ville, le town centre
ces (mpl/fpl) these/those
cette (f) this
chaise, la chair
chaise-longue, la deck-chair
chalet, le chalet/cottage
chambre, la bedroom
champ, le field
championnat, le championship
change, le exchange
changer to change
charcuterie, la pork butcher's/cold meat
charge, la cost/tax
chasseur, le hunter
château, le castle
chaud/e hot/warm
chaudière, la boiler
chauffage (central), le (central) heating
chaussette, la sock
chaussure, la shoe
chemin, le way/path
chemise, la shirt
chèque, le cheque
cher/chère dear/expensive
cheval, le horse
cheville, la ankle
chose, la thing

cintre, le hanger
cirque, le circus
clair/e light (colour)
classique classical
clavicule, la collarbone
clé, la key
clientèle, la customers
climatisation, la air conditioning
club, le club
coca, le Coca-cola
cochon, le pig
codes, les (mpl) dipped lights
cœur, le heart
coffre-fort, le safe deposit box
cognac, le brandy
coiffure, la hairdressing/hair style
coin, le corner
collant, le tights
collier, le necklace
colonne vertébrale, la spine
combien how much/how many
commander to order
comme as/like
comment how
commissariat, le police station
commission, la commission
commotion cérébrale, la concussion
complet full/wholemeal
composter to validate a ticket
comprendre to understand
comprimé, le tablet
compris/e included/understood
compteur, le meter
concert, le concert
concession, la concession
conduire to drive
conserves, les (fpl) tinned food
constipé/e constipated
contagieux/gieuse contagious
continuer to continue/carry on
contre against
corbeille, la basket
cornet, le cornet
correspondance, la connection
corsage, le blouse
côte, la rib/coast
coton, le cotton
cou, le neck
couche, la nappy/layer

couleur, la colour
coup de soleil, le sunburn
coupe, la goblet/dish/cup (sport)
coupé/e cut
courant, le current
courir to run
couronne, la crown
courroie, la belt
cours, le course/lesson/flow
course, la race/errand
court/e short
couteau, le knife
couvert, le plate setting
couverture, la blanket
cravate, la tie
crédit, le credit
crème, la cream
crème, le white coffee
crevaison, la puncture
cric, le jack (car)
crise de foie, la indigestion
croisement, le junction
cuillère, la spoon
cuir, le leather
cuisine, la kitchen/cuisine
cuisinière, la cooker
cuisse, la thigh
cure-dents, le toothpick
cycliste, le/la cyclist

d'accord agreed
d'où from where
dame, la lady
dans in
date, la date (day)
de of/from
de rien Don't mention it/You're welcome
dedans inside/in it/in them
défense de forbidden
défilé, le parade
dégustation, la food/wine tasting
déjeuner, le midday meal
délicieux/euse delicious
demain tomorrow
démarrer to start up (car)
demie, la half
demi-heure, la half an hour
demi-pension, la half board
dent, la tooth
dentelle, la lace

entifrice, le toothpaste
entiste, le dentist
épannage, le breakdown service
éranger to disturb
ériveur, le sailing dinghy
ernier/dernière last
errière behind
es, (pl) some/any
escendre to go down/get
ff/take down
escente, la descent/downhill
ésirer to desire/want
ésolé/e sorry
essert, le dessert
evant in front of
évelopper to develop
abétique diabetic
abolo, le lemonade drink with
rup
apositive, la slide (photo)
arrhée, la diarrhoea
rection, la direction/steering
scothèque, la discotheque
sque, le record
straction, la entertainment
s, le back
ouble, le copy/double
ouche, la shower
ouzaine, la dozen
agée, la sugared almond
ap, le bed sheet
oit/e straight
oite right
  some/any/of the/from the
ur/e hard
rer to last

au, l' (f) water
au de Javel, l' (f) bleach
au-de-vie, l' (f) brandy
chappement, l' (m) exhaust (car)
cole, l' (f) school
crire to write
ffort, l' (m) effort
glise, l' (f) church
astique, l' (m) elastics/bunjee
 mp)
ectricité, l' (f) electricity
mbrayage, l' (m) clutch
mplacement, l' (m) pitch/place

emporter to take away
en in/of it/of them
en face opposite
en panne out of order
enceinte pregnant
enchanté/e delighted
encore again/still
enfant, l' (m/f) child
entier/entière whole
entorse, l' (f) sprain
entrer to enter
entracte, l' (m) interval (theatre)
environ about/approximately
envoyer to send
épaule, l' (f) shoulder
épicé/e spicy
épicerie, l' (f) grocer's shop
épilepsie, l' (f) epilepsy
épileptique epileptic
épreuve, l' (f) print (photo)
équitation, l' (f) horse riding
erreur, l' (f) mistake
escalier, l' (m) stairs
escalier roulant, l' (m) escalator
espèces (fpl) cash
esquimau, l' (m) choc ice on
stick/Eskimo
essayer to try
essence, l' (f) petrol
est, l' (m) East
est is
estomac, l' (m) stomach
et and
étage, l' (m) storey/level
étudiant/e, l' (m/f) student
excellent/e excellent
excuser to excuse
exposition, l' (f) exhibition

faire to do/make
faites le plein fill up (petrol)
femme, la woman/wife
fenêtre, la window
fer, le iron
ferme, la farm
fermer to close
fesse, la buttock
festival, le festival
fête, la feast/festivity
fête foraine, la fun fair
feu, le fire/traffic light

feuille, la leaf/sheet (paper)
feuille de soins, la treatment sheet
feux, les (mpl) lights/fires
ficelle, la narrow French loaf/string
fiche, la form
fille, la girl/daughter
filtre, le filter
finir to finish
flacon, le small bottle
flotteur, le armband/float
flûte, la narrow French loaf/flute
foie, le liver
foire, la fair
fois (une/deux) once/twice
foncé/e dark colour
foot(ball), le football
forcer to force/to break into
forfait, le set price/all-in deal
fort/e strong
foulard, le scarf
fracture, la fracture/break
frais (m)/fraîche (f) fresh/cool
franc, le franc
français/e French
frappé iced (coffee)
frein, le brake
froid/e cold
fromage, le cheese
fruit, le fruit
fumer to smoke
fumeur, le smoker

galerie, la gallery
garage, le garage
gardé/e guarded/secure
gare, la station
garer/se garer to park
garni/e/s garnished
gâteau, le cake
gauche, la left
gaufrette, la wafer
gaz, le gas
gazeux/euse fizzy
général/e general
généraliste, le general practioner/ doctor
genou, le knee
gentil/le kind
gilet, le (de sauvetage) life jacket

glace, la ice/ice-cream
glacier, le ice-cream parlour/glacier
glaçon, le ice cube/icicle
golf, le golf
gorge, la throat/gorge
goûter to taste
grand/e tall/large
gratuit/e free of charge
grave serious
gravillons, les (mpl) loose chippings
grippe, la 'flu/influenza
gris/e grey
gros/se big/large
gueule de bois, la hangover
guichet, le ticket office/counter
guide, le guide/guide book

haut/e high
hecto, l' (m) 100 grammes
heure, l' (f) hour/time/o'clock
hier yesterday
homme, l' (m) man
hôpital, l' (m) hospital
horaire, l' (m) time table
hôte, l' (m) host/guest/patron
hôtel, l' (m) hotel
huilier, l' (m) oil/vinegar cruet
hygiénique hygienic

ici here
il y a there is/there are
il faut it is necessary
illimité/e unlimited
immatriculation, l' (f) registration
immobilière, l'agence estate age
inclus/e included
indigestion, l' (f) indigestion
infection, l' (f) infection
infusion, l' (f) herbal tea
insecte, l' (m) insect
insecticide, l' (m) insect repelle
insolation, l' (f) sunstroke
interdit forbidden
intéressant/e interesting

j'ai I have
jamais never
jambe, la leg
jambon, le ham

118

rdin, le garden
une yellow
|
une young
unesse, la youth
li/e pretty
uer to play
uet, le toy
ur, le day
urnal, le newspaper
pe, la skirt
s, le juice
squ'à/au/aux up to/until

o, le kilogramme

the/it/her
there
bas over there
ne, la wool
sser to leave behind/to allow
t, le milk
npe, la lamp
ague, la tongue
abo, le washbasin
the/it/him
er/légère light/weak drink
t/e slow
tement slowly
tille, la lentil/lens
quel which one
s (pl) the
ssive, la washing
tre, la letter
er to lift
rairie, la bookshop
re free
re-service, le self-service
ne, la line
ge, le linen/clothing
ueur, la liqueur
uide, le liquid
le bed
e, le litre
re, la pound
e, le book
ation, la hiring
e, la box (theatre)
a far
sirs, les leisure
g/ue long

longtemps a long time
louer to hire/rent/let
lourd/e heavy
loyer, le rent
luge, la sledge
lumière, la light
lunettes, les (fpl) glasses

Madame (f) Mrs/Madam
Mademoiselle (f) Miss
magasin, le shop
maillot (de bain), le swimsuit
main, la hand
mais but
maison, la house/homemade/family firm
mal badly
mal, le pain/ache/sickness
mal de mer, le sea sickness
malheureusement unfortunately
manche, la sleeve
Manche, la English Channel
manger to eat
manteau, le coat/overcoat
marchand, le shopkeeper
marché, le market/deal
marcher to walk/to function
marée, la tide
mari, le husband
marié/e married
marionnette, la puppet
marmelade, la marmalade
maroquinerie, la leather goods
marque, la brand
marron, le brown/chestnut
masque, le mask
matelas, le mattress
matin, le morning
matinée, la morning/afternoon performance
mauvais/e bad
me me
médecin, le doctor
médicament, le medicine
même same/even
ménager/ménagère household
menu, le menu
mer, la sea
merci thank you
mère, la mother
mettre to put

midi midday/noon
mie, la white (of bread loaf)
milkshake, le milkshake
mille-feuilles, le cream vanilla slice
minuit midnight
moi me
moins less/to (time)
mois, le month
moitié, la half
monnaie, la (small) change
Monsieur Mr/Sir
montre, la watch
montrer to show
morceau, le piece
motif, le pattern
mou/molle soft
mouchoir, le handkerchief
mousseux, le sparkling wine
mûr/e ripe
musée, le museum
musique, la music

n'est pas is not
nager to swim
nappe, la tablecloth
nature plain/natural
nausée, la nausea
nautique nautical
navette, la shuttle
ne . . . jamais never
ne . . . pas not
ne . . . personne nobody
ne . . . plus no more/no longer
ne . . . que only
ne . . . rien nothing
nectarine, la nectarine
neuf/neuve brand new
nez, le nose
ni . . . ni neither . . . nor
night club, le night club
Noël (m/f) Christmas
noir/e black
nom, le name
non no
nord, le North
note, la bill/musical note
nouveau/nouvelle new
nuit, la night
nuitée, la overnight stay
numéro, le number

numéroté/e numbered

obtenir to obtain
occupé/e occupied
œil, l' (m) eye
on one/someone/we
ont (p111) they have
opération, l' (f) operation
orange, l' (f) orange
orangeade, l' (f) fizzy orange
orchestre, l' (m) orchestra/stall (theatre)
ordonnance, l' (f) prescription
ordures, les (fpl) rubbish
oreille, l' (f) ear
oreillons, les (mpl) mumps
os, l' (m) bone
otite, l' (f) ear infection
ou or
où where
oublier to forget
ouest, l' (m) West
oui yes
ouvert/e opened/open
ouvrir to open

paille, la straw
pain, le bread/loaf
palme, la flipper
panne, la breakdown
pansement, le dressing (medical)
pantalon, le trousers
papeterie, la stationner's
papier, le paper
paquet, le packet
par by/per
parasol, le parasol
parc, le park
pardon sorry
pare-brise, le wind screen
pare-chocs, le bumper
parfum, le perfume/flavour
parler (p111) to speak
partir to go away/leave
pas not
pas de not any/no
passeport, le passport
passer to pass/to spend (time)
patinoire, la ice rink
patins, les (mpl) skates
pâtisserie, la cake shop/cakes

atron, le owner/boss
ayer to pay
ays, le country/local region
éage, le toll
êche, la peach/fishing
édale, la pedal
einture, la painting/paint
ellicule, la film (camera)
ension, la guest house/board
erdre to lose
ermis, le licence
ersonne, la person
étanque, la petanque (bowls
ame)
etit/e small
eu little (small amount)
eut/peux can
hare, le headlight/light house
armacie, la chemist's shop
ied, le foot
éton, le pedestrian
le, la battery (e.g. torch)
ng-pong, le table tennis
qué/e stung
qûre, la sting/injection
scine, la swimming pool
ste, la track/ski run
ace, la seat/town square
age, la beach
aît, s'il vous please
an, le plan/map
anche, la board/plank
anche à voile, la windsurfing
aquette, la small flat packet
at, le dish
ein/e full
omb, le lead
ombage, le tooth filling
ongée, la diving
ongée sous-marine, la scuba
ving
us more
us tard later
eu, le tyre
eumatique inflatable
eumonie, la pneumonia
ids, le weight
ids lourd, le heavy goods
hicle
ignet, le wrist
nture, la shoe size

poisson, le fish
poitrine, la chest/bust
pommade, la ointment
pont, le bridge
porc, le pork/pig
port, le harbour
porte, la door
porte-clés, le key ring
porte-monnaie, le purse
portefeuille, le wallet
portière, la door (train/car)
portion, la portion
porto, le port
pose, la exposure (photo)
postal/e postal
poste, la post office
pot, le jar/jug
potable drinkable/safe to drink
poumon, le lung
pour for/in order to
prendre to take
près near
présenter to introduce
préservatif, le condom
pressé/e in a hurry/squeezed
pression, la draught
beer/pressure
prêt/e ready
pris taken
prochain/e next
proche near
produit, le product
profond/e deep
profondeur, la depth
programme, le programme
provisoire temporary
public/que public
Publifax, le fax machine for public
use
puis then
pull, le pullover

quai, le platform
quand when
quart, le quarter
quartier, le neighbourhood
que that/what/whom
quel/le which?
quelqu'un someone/somebody
qui who/which/whom
quincaillerie, la hardware (store)

qu'est-ce que c'est? what is it?
qu'est-ce qu'il y a? what is there ?

radiateur, le radiator
ralentir to slow down
ramasser to pick up
rame, la oar
randonnée pédestre, la hiking/rambling
rappel, le reminder
raquette, la racket
rasoir, le razor
rayon, le shelf/shop department
recommander to recommend
reçu, le receipt
redevance, la fee
réfléchir to reflect/to think about
régate, la regatta
régional/e regional
règlement, le rule
règles, les (fpl) (woman's) period
rempart, le city wall
remplir to fill
rendez-vous, le appointment
repas, le meal
repos, le rest
réservation, la reservation
réserver to reserve
restaurant, le restaurant
reste, le rest
rester to remain/stay
revenir to come back
rez-de-chaussée, le ground floor/first floor (USA)
rhume, le head cold
rideau, le curtain
rien nothing
risque, le risk
riverains, les (mpl) local residents
robe, la dress
robinet, le (water) tap
rond-point, le roundabout
rose pink
roue, la wheel
rouge red
rougeole, la measles
rougeur, la rash
route, la road
rubéole, la German measles
rue, la street

s'appeler to be called
s'arrêter to stop (oneself)
s'il vous plaît (if you) please
sable, le sand
sac, le bag
sac de couchage, le sleeping bag
sac à dos, le ruck sack
saison, la season
salle, la room
salle à manger, la dining room
salle de bains, la bathroom
salon, le salon/drawing room
sandwich, le sandwich
sans without
satisfait/e satisfied
sauter to jump
savon, le soap
sculpture, la sculpture
secours, le rescue
séjour, le stay
self-service, le self-service
semaine, la week
sentir to smell/to feel/to sense
serré/e tight/strong coffee
serrez à droite keep to the right
serrure, la lock
service, le service
serviette, la napkin/towel/briefcase
se trouver to be situated
seulement only
shampooing, le shampoo
sinusite, la sinus infection
sirop, le syrup
ski, le skiing
ski de fond, le cross country skiing
ski nautique, le water skiing
soie, la silk
soir, le evening
solaire for the sun
soleil, le sun
somnolence, la drowsiness
sorte, la type/sort
sortie, la exit
sortir to go out
sous-sol, le basement
sous-titre, le sub title
spécialité, la speciality
spiritueux, les (mpl) spirits (drinks)

ort, le sport
ade, le stadium
ation-service, la petrol station
ationnement, le parking
ores, les (mpl) blinds
cette, la lollipop
cre, le sugar
d, le South
pplément, le supplement
ppositoire, le suppository
r on
rgelés, les (mpl) frozen food
s, en extra

bac, le tobacco
ble d'hôte, la evening meal
ovided
rd late
rif, le tariff/price
sse, la cup
ux, le rate
xes, les (fpl) taxes
xi, le taxi
écarte, la telephone card
éphérique, le cable car
éphone, le telephone
mpérature, la temperature/fever
mps, le time (general)/weather
rrain, le pitch/site
te, la head
é, le tea
rs, le third (quantity)
mbre, le stamp
e-bouchon, le corkscrew
e-fesses le ski tow
er to pull
lettes, les (fpl) toilets
ur, le tour
ur, la tower
urner to turn
urnoi, le tournament
s (mpl)/toutes (fpl) all
t/e everything/all (sing)
t de suite at once
t droit straight on
ux, la cough
nche, la slice
nquille quiet
veller, le traveller's cheque
versée, la crossing

traverser to cross
travail, le job/work
très very
trop too much
trouver to find

ulcère, l' (m) ulcer
un/e a/one
uni/e plain/united

vacances, les (fpl) holidays
vapeur, la steam/steamed
varappe, la rock climbing
varicelle, la chicken pox
végétalien/ne vegan
végétarien/ne vegetarian
vélo, le bicycle
vendre to sell
venir to come
ventre, le tummy/belly
verre, le glass
version française, la dubbed foreign film
version originale, la original language film
vert/e green
vertige, le dizziness/vertigo
vestiaire, le cloakroom
vêtement, le garment
viande, la meat
vieux/vieille old
ville, la town
vin, le wine
vite quickly
vitesse, la speed/gear (car)
voilà there/here it is
voile, la sail/veil
voir to see
voiture, la car
vol, le flight/theft
volant, le driving wheel
voler to steal/to fly
volet, le shutter
vomir to vomit
voyage, le journey

wagon-lit, le sleeping car

yeux, les (mpl) eyes

Titles available

For a complete languages catalogue please contact:
BBC Books, Book Service By Post,
PO Box 29,
Douglas,
Isle of Man, IM99 1BQ,
tel: 01624-675137, fax: 01624-70923

BBC books are available at all good bookshops or direct
from the publishers as above.